GLOBAL STUDIES SERIES

FOCUS ON

South & Southeast Asia

GLOBE FEARON EDUCATIONAL PUBLISHER
A Division of Simon & Schuster
Upper Saddle River, New Jersey

Director of Editorial and Marketing, Secondary Supplementary: Nancy Surridge
Project Editors: Karen Bernhaut and Lynn Kloss
Marketing Manager: Rhonda Anderson
Production Director: Kurt Scherwatzky
Production Editor: Alan Dalgleish
Editorial Development: WestEd, Ink
Art Director: Pat Smythe
Electronic Page Production: Margarita Giammanco
Photo Research: Jenifer Hixson
Interior Design: Margarita Giammanco
Cover Design: Marsha Cohen
Cover Art: Owen Jones

Grateful acknowledgment is made to the following for illustrations, photographs, and reproductions on the pages indicated.

Photo credits: **p. 1:** Ron Chapple/FPG; **p. 3:** Sean Sprague/Impact Visuals; **p. 4:** Courtesy of the United Nations; **p. 7:** Sid Lathan/Photo Researchers; **p. 9:** Travelpix, FPG; **p. 11:** Tom Sawyer, FPG; **p. 11:** Courtesy of Standard Oil Company; **p. 12:** M. Bryan Ginsberg; **p. 16:** Suzanne L. Murphy, FPG; **p. 16:** Steve Vidler, Nawrocki Stock Photo; **p. 17:** Travelpix, FPG; **p. 17:** Jean Kugler, FPG; **p. 21:** Ray Garner, FPG: **p. 23:** Josef Beck, FPG; **p. 25:** Richard Harrington, FPG; **p. 28:** Corbis, Bettmann; **p. 30:** Henri Cartier-Bresson, Magnum; **p. 33:** Sean Sprague, Impact Visuals; **p. 35:** Sean Sprague, Impact Visuals; **p. 36:** M. Bryan Ginsberg; **p. 38:** Marilyn Silverstone, Magnum Photos Inc.; **p. 41:** The United Nations; **p. 43:** Baldev, Sygma; **p. 44:** The United Nations: **p. 46:** UPI/Corbis, Bettmann; **p. 47:** Baldev, Sygma; **p. 50:** UPI/Corbis, Bettmann; **p. 53:** M. Bryan Ginsberg; **p. 55:** J. Messerschmidt, FPG; **p. 58:** The Granger Collection; **p. 61:** Charles Marden Fitch, FPG; **p. 63:** Corbis, Bettmann; **p. 64:** Jason Bleitreu, Sygma; **p. 65:** Jacques Langevin, Sygma; **p. 67:** Werner Foreman Collection, Art Resource; **p. 71:** Jacques Langevin, Sygma; **p. 73:** Jacques Langevin, Sygma; **p. 74:** David Austin, Tony Stone; **p. 75:** Reuters/Corbis, Bettmann; **p. 77:** Sergio Dorantes, Sygma; **p. 78:** Sydney H. Schamberg, The New York Times; **p. 81:** Arthur D'Arazien, The Image Bank; **p. 85:** Joe Vissel, Tony Stone Images; **p. 87:** Corbis, Bettmann; **p. 88:** Telegraph Color Library, FPG; **p. 90:** Bruno Berry, Magnum

Copyright © 1997 by Globe Fearon Educational Publisher, a division of Simon & Schuster, One Lake Street, Upper Saddle River, New Jersey 07458. All rights reserved. No part of this book may be reproduced or transmitted in any form or by any means, electronic or mechanical, including photocopying, recording, or by any information storage and retrieval system, without permission in writing from the publisher.

Printed in the United States of America 2 3 4 5 6 7 8 9 10   00 99 98 97

ISBN 0-835-91941-2

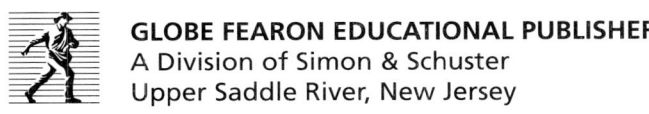

GLOBE FEARON EDUCATIONAL PUBLISHER
A Division of Simon & Schuster
Upper Saddle River, New Jersey

CONTENTS

INTRODUCTION		**The World and Its Cultures**	**1**
Section	1	Focus on Cultures	2
Section	2	Focus on Places	6
Section	3	Focus on Change	8
CHAPTER 1		**The Land and People of South and Southeast Asia**	**9**
Section	1	The Lands of South and Southeast Asia	10
Case Study	1	*Waiting for the Rain*	18
Section	2	The People	19
		Reviewing Chapter 1	**20**
CHAPTER 2		**The History of South Asia**	**21**
Section	1	An Ancient Heritage: Early Civilizations of India	22
Section	2	Europeans Arrive	27
Section	3	India Wins Independence	29
Case Study	2	*Salt March for Freedom*	31
		Reviewing Chapter 2	**32**
CHAPTER 3		**Changing Patterns of Life in South Asia**	**33**
Section	1	India: A Land of Tradition and Change	34
Section	2	India: Future Trends	35
Section	3	The Arts and Literature in South Asia	37
Case Study	3	*The Hollywood of India*	39
		Reviewing Chapter 3	**40**
CHAPTER 4		**South Asia in the World Today**	**41**
Section	1	India's Government and Economy	42
Section	2	Other Nations of South Asia	45
Section	3	South Asia and the World	48
Case Study	4	*Benazir Bhutto: The First Islamic Woman Leader*	51
		Reviewing Chapter 4	**52**
CHAPTER 5		**The Heritage of Southeast Asia**	**53**
Section	1	Early Civilizations of Southeast Asia	54
Section	2	Europeans Colonize the Region	56
Case Study	5	*The Myths of Indonesia*	57
Section	3	Southeast Asians Fight for Freedom	59
		Reviewing Chapter 5	**62**

CHAPTER 6		**Changing Patterns of Life in Southeast Asia**	**63**
Section	1	Patterns of Life in Southeast Asia	64
Section	2	Arts and Literature in Southeast Asia	67
Case Study	6	*Preserving a Great Heritage: The Ancient Capital of Angkor*	69
		Reviewing Chapter 6	**70**
CHAPTER 7		**Southeast Asia in the World Today**	**71**
Section	1	The Economy of Southeast Asia	72
Section	2	Political Trends in Southeast Asia	75
Section	3	Southeast Asia and the World	76
Case Study	7	*Return to the Killing Fields*	79
		Reviewing Chapter 7	**80**
CHAPTER 8		**AUSTRALIA, NEW ZEALAND, AND OCEANIA**	**81**
Section	1	The Land and People of Australia and New Zealand	82
Section	2	Australia and New Zealand: From Colonies to Independent Nations	86
Section	3	Oceania: A World of Pacific Islands	89
Case Study	8	*The Aborigines: Caught Between Two Worlds*	92
		Reviewing Chapter 8	**93**

MAP OF SOUTH ASIA	**94**
MAP OF SOUTHEAST ASIA	**95**
GLOSSARY	**96**
INDEX	**98**
MAPS, CHARTS, AND GRAPHS	
South and Southeast Asia's Physical Features	10
South and Southeast Asia's Climates	14
Buddhism and Hinduism to A.D. 500	24
Countries of South Asia	34
Religion in South Asia	45
Southeast Asia Under Foreign Control to 1914	60
Countries of Southeast Asia	72
Map of Australia, New Zealand, and Oceania	83
Some Facts About Australia, New Zealand, and Oceania	84
Map of South Asia	94
Map of Southeast Asia	95

INTRODUCTION

The World and Its Cultures

Why is it important to learn about the world's cultures?

One aspect of culture is the way people relate to each other. Teenagers in the United States tend to relate to each other in casual ways. What does this tell us about their culture?

Looking at Key Terms

- **culture** the way of life of a group of people, including their ideas, customs, skills, and arts
- **cultural diversity** having a variety of cultures
- **global village** a term that refers to the entire modern world where diverse people communicate, share experiences, and depend on one another for resources
- **extended family** the family unit in most traditional societies, consisting of three or four generations living in one household
- **nuclear family** the family unit in most developed societies, consisting often of a father, mother, and children
- **cultural diffusion** the spread of new ideas and new ways of doing things from one society to others
- **interdependent** the state of being dependent on one another for support or survival

On Assignment...

Formulating Questions: Asking good questions will help you determine the main ideas of subjects you study. As you read this chapter, write questions you would like answered about South and Southeast Asia. Look for On Assignment hint boxes to help you formulate your questions. When you are finished reading the chapter, you will finalize your list of questions.

SECTION 1

Focus on Cultures

To what extent does culture determine who we are and how we behave?

- In the United States, people greet one another by shaking hands. In Thailand, people greet one another by bowing low, with their palms pressed together.
- People in some societies, such as the Muslims of Pakistan, do not eat pork. People in other societies, such as the Hindus of India, do not eat beef.
- In some places, such as the United States, people measure wealth by the size of their homes. In other places, such as Papua New Guinea, wealth is measured by the number of pigs a person owns.

A World of Many Cultures

All these differences are differences between **cultures**. Culture is the way of life of a group of people. You may think of culture as what people add to the natural world. All people have a culture.

The people who share a particular culture may or may not live in a single country. For example, people of the Jewish faith live in many countries of the world, including the United States, South Africa, Mexico, and Israel.

One country may contain more than one culture. The United States is a country with people from many different cultures. Therefore, we say that the United States is a country of **cultural diversity**.

The cultural diversity of the United States provides a good reason for us to learn about other parts of the world. By learning about different world cultures, we learn more about ourselves. We learn to appreciate the richness of our heritage.

The World as a Global Village You may have heard people say that the world is becoming a smaller place every day. What they mean is that it is becoming easier to communicate with people around the world. Recent advances in technology have made communication and transportation much easier. As an example, consider the journey of Ferdinand Magellan—the first person to sail completely around the world. In the 1500s, Magellan's journey took three years. Today, airplanes can circle the globe in less than 24 hours. During the American Revolution, it took months for letters from the leaders of the 13 colonies to reach leaders in England. Today, world leaders can communicate instantly by using the telephone, fax, or Internet.

All these changes have created a world that many people refer to as a **global village**. This term refers to the way in which diverse people from around the world communicate, share experiences, and depend on one another for resources.

What Is Culture? When some people think of culture, they think of a symphony orchestra or a dance festival. Culture embraces far more than the arts, however. For instance, if you put on jeans in the morning, listen to rock music, go to school five days a week, and watch football games on television on weekends, you are participating in U.S. culture. On the other hand, if you herd cattle, speak the Setswana language, play soccer, and wear tribal garments, you might be part of the Tswana culture in Botswana.

Culture examines how humans live on earth. It answers such questions as:

- What is family life like in a certain culture?
- How do the people of a certain culture make a living?
- What religions do the people of a certain culture practice?

- What sort of government do they have?
- How does their culture affect the way they interact with the land?

Learning a Culture Culture is learned. However, it is not learned the way you learn algebra or biology. You begin learning your culture the minute you are born. You learn to eat certain foods, wear certain clothes, and speak a certain language. You learn appropriate ways to behave. You learn certain beliefs and customs.

Beliefs and Customs Every culture has specific beliefs and customs. For example, in many Asian cultures, people believe that it is the sons' responsibility to care for their parents as they age. Therefore, families tend to be large. This increases the chance that there will be many sons. Generally, the beliefs and customs of a culture are deeply related to its religion.

Religion Most cultures have religions. Religion is a belief in a superhuman power or powers to be obeyed and worshipped as creators and rulers of the universe. A religion usually includes a set of beliefs and practices that govern behavior. Examples of religions around the world are Christianity, Islam, Judaism, Hinduism, and Buddhism.

Members of a religious group hold similar beliefs about how people should treat one another. They hold similar beliefs about how the world came into existence. Many religious groups believe that there is some kind of life after death.

Language A shared language is one of the most important elements of a culture. Without it, people in a culture would not be able to communicate.

All cultures have languages. These languages express thoughts, beliefs, feelings, and questions. Most people are born with the ability to learn to speak a language. However, the actual language they speak is determined by their culture.

Family Organization In most cultures, the family is the most important unit of life. The family teaches young people how they are expected to behave.

In many cultures, three or four generations of a family live together in a single home or compound. This type of family organization is known as the **extended family**.

In traditional farming societies, a large extended family is necessary to help the family meet its needs. The young and middle-aged men and women of the family farm the land, while older members often look after and teach the children. In other

The nuclear family, such as this one in Thailand, includes a wife, a husband, and their children. Nuclear families can be large or small, depending on the number of children.

Introduction

In traditional societies, families or villages produce nearly all that they need to survive. In northern Nigeria, villagers trade or sell bowls they have made and goods they have grown.

societies, the extended family is a sign of the culture's respect for its elderly. Families are expected to live with and care for their older members.

In some cultures, the typical family includes a wife, husband, and their children. This organization is known as the **nuclear family**. The nuclear family is common in developed countries. Developed countries have economies based on industry and technology. Families in developed countries often do not need to be large to meet the needs of everyday living. However, a nuclear family is not necessarily small. A nuclear family can have many children.

Economies and Governments

All societies have economic and political systems. Economic systems determine what goods should be produced, how much should be produced, and what the goods are worth. Political systems are ways of organizing government.

Ways of Meeting Economic Needs In traditional societies, families or villages produce nearly all the goods they need to survive. The members of these societies hunt and farm for food. They make their own clothes and build their own homes. If they produce more than they need, they might trade what is left over for other goods.

In modern societies, individuals tend to specialize in the type of work they do. Because people do not make all that they need, they use money to buy and sell goods and services.

Whether a society is traditional or modern, it has to deal with the scarcity of resources. *Scarcity* means "not enough." In economics, it refers to the availability of natural resources, such as water, or resources made by humans, such as housing. Reasons for scarcity vary. For example, food can be scarce if a region has been hit by drought. Sometimes, one group in society gains power and purposely makes resources scarce for another group.

The economies of many modern societies are organized into free enterprise systems. People are able to start and run almost any business they choose. The governments of such countries make few decisions about what is produced and how much it costs.

Some countries organize their economies in a way called central planning. Here, the government makes almost all of the decisions about what goods are produced and how much they will cost. Governments that use central planning usually own and operate most of the nation's industries.

Most nations today, including the United States, have mixed economies. In a mixed economy, private ownership of business is combined with government control. A mixed economy allows the government to make laws to control the economy and protect the public. Most businesses are owned by individuals and will succeed or fail based on their ability to make a profit.

Government When people live together, they need rules and laws for solving problems. Governments serve this purpose. Governments are made up of people who have the power to create and enforce the rules and laws of society.

There are various ways to organize a government. Below, you will read about three types of governments: democracies, monarchies, and dictatorships.

In a democracy, citizens have the right to participate in government. In many democracies, citizens vote for people to represent them in government. This is the way democracy works in the United States. The main feature of a democracy is that people have the power to shape their government through voting or other means.

In a monarchy, a king or queen heads the government and holds absolute power. Heredity determines who holds the crown. Today, a number of countries have constitutional monarchies. In a constitutional monarchy, the king or queen holds little real power. A body of elected officials, such as a parliament, makes the laws. Britain has such a government.

In a dictatorship, a leader or a group holds power by force. People who express their opposition to the government are usually punished harshly. The country of Iraq is a dictatorship ruled by Saddam Hussein.

Cultures Change Cultures are always changing, although some cultures change faster than others. U.S. culture has changed rapidly in recent years. Other cultures have had few changes in hundreds of years. For example, among the San people of Africa's Kalahari Desert, ways of life have changed little. The San still use simple tools in gathering wild plants and hunting animals.

Cultures borrow items or ideas from other cultures. Blue jeans are an example of this borrowing. Jeans were originally developed in San Francisco in the mid-1800s. These sturdy pants originally were made for gold miners. Less than 100 years later, people all over the globe wear jeans for comfort and for fashion.

Cultural Diffusion The spread of new ideas and new ways of doing things from one society to others is called **cultural diffusion**. The popularity of reggae music is an example of cultural diffusion. Reggae music began in Jamaica. In the 1970s, Bob Marley and other musicians played reggae to audiences in the United States and Europe. The popularity of reggae spread and influenced the rock music of the 1980s, especially in Britain.

A Global System

The world relies on a global economic system. Valuable resources such as oil and iron are not spread evenly. One place might be rich in many resources. Another might be rich in only one. Therefore, the people of the world must trade with one another to meet their needs.

People rely on one another for more than just goods and services. As you read earlier, the world is sometimes called a global village. It can also be said that the people of the world are **interdependent**. *Interdependent* means "people depend on one another." An event on one side of the globe can affect lives on the other side.

With interdependence comes responsibility. Today, conflict between faraway cultures can affect our lives. By understanding other cultures, we can make the differences that separate us count less and the similarities

> **On Assignment...**
>
> At this point, you may be wondering about the cultures of South and Southeast Asia. Write down five questions about these cultures that you would like answered by the time you have finished this book.

that connect us count more. By cooperating with one another, we can keep our world at peace and in balance.

Section 1 Review

1. What is culture?
2. **Inferring** The United States is often called a multicultural society. The prefix *multi-* means "many." What do you think multicultural means? Why do you think the United States is called a multicultural society?

SECTION 2

Focus on Places

How does a knowledge of geography help in understanding world cultures?

Geography, especially cultural geography, is an important part of global studies. Understanding where people live helps to create an understanding of who they are and why their culture developed as it did.

Two questions geographers ask are:
- Where do people live?
- Why do they live there?

To answer these questions, geographers look at five basic themes—location, place, interaction, movement, and regions.

Location

To study a place, geographers begin by finding out where it is located. A place's location is its position on the earth's surface. Location can be expressed in two ways: absolute location and relative location.

Absolute location is an exact, precise place on the earth. You give an absolute location when you use longitude and latitude. For example, New York City's absolute location is 41° North, 74° West.

Relative location is where a place is in relation to other places. You give a relative location when you say you live 12 miles (19 km) southeast of Columbus, Ohio.

Place

All places on the earth have distinct features that make them unique. Geographers use natural features and cultural features to describe places.

Natural Features When you visit a place, you might notice the sandy beaches, the warm weather, and the tall palm trees. These are natural, or physical, features. Another way to think of natural features is to think of them as the environment.

Take a special look at the environment of places you study because the environment affects how people live. You can identify environment if you look at climate, land, and water.

Climate includes all the elements that make up the weather over a period of time—especially precipitation, temperature, and wind. Climate influences the kinds of crops that grow in a certain region and the type of homes and buildings people make there. It determines the clothing people wear and the types of work people can do.

Land includes the soil, vegetation, mountains, and mineral resources of a region. Land affects crops, animal life, and the work people do.

Water is the third essential part of the environment. Water includes rivers, lakes, and oceans. Water is a vital part of all people's lives. Without it there can be no farming or irrigation. Water can aid transportation and it powers electrical generators.

Cultural Features When you visit a city or country, you might talk about it by describing its delicious food or by describing graceful old buildings that stand by a river. These are cultural features.

Cultural features are the part of the landscape that people add. When you know something about the natural and cultural features of a place, you know what makes it different from other places on earth.

Interaction

The theme of interaction helps geographers understand the relationship between people and their environment.

Every place on earth has advantages and disadvantages for the people who live there. Usually places with many advantages contain large populations. These places are often near water and are flat enough for easy farming. Other advantages might include an abundance of natural resources that can build an economy.

Fewer people live where it proves more difficult to survive. But people are problem solvers and find ways to interact with their environment. Humans have learned to build aqueducts to bring water to dry areas. They have also carved terraces into mountains so that they can farm the land.

Movement

Geographers use the theme of movement to find out how people, ideas, and products move from place to place.

Many places are made up of people who have moved there from other places. Movement explains why many Vietnamese people live in Texas and California. Some people move because they want to live somewhere with better job opportunities or because they want to escape from a bad situation.

Movement explains the worldwide popularity of blue jeans. Products move when people want something that they do not have. Movement also shows how the religion of Islam spread from the Arabian Peninsula to Africa, Asia, and the United States. Goods and ideas move when people move.

The theme of movement helps you to understand how and why people from one place in the world interact with people from many other areas.

Region

The basic unit of geographic study is the region. A region is a part of the world that has natural or cultural features distinct from

> **On Assignment...**
> What would you like to know about the relationship of people and the environment in South and Southeast Asia? Think of questions you would like to ask.

People of all cultures are affected by the environment in which they live. These nomads of southern Jordan have found ways to adapt to the vast desert that is their home.

Introduction 7

other regions. The study of regions helps you compare areas of the world. It helps you to see the earth as a system of places that are related in different ways.

You are probably most familiar with political regions. A nation, state, or city is a political region. Regions can be defined by other natural or cultural features. For example, Florida is part of a plains region, a tourist region, and a tropical climate region.

Section 2 Review

1. What are the five themes of geography? How do they help organize the study of geography?
2. **Analyzing** Why is an understanding of geography important in global studies?

SECTION 3

Focus on Change

What changes affect the world's environment?

Geographers and scientists are often called upon to guess the changes that may occur in a region. Predicting these changes helps people plan for the future, avoid catastrophes, and make wise use of resources. One thing geographers and scientists cannot do is stop change from happening.

Some changes result from new inventions and new ways of doing things. For example, fertilizers, pesticides, and farm machines have changed how food is grown. Jets and bullet trains have sped up transportation. Computers have changed how people work and communicate.

Change can be both good and bad. Chemical fertilizers and insecticides improve crop yield but may damage the environments in which birds and fish live. Jets greatly decrease travel time but cause air pollution and noise pollution. Computers and computer-controlled robots make work more efficient but may cause people to lose jobs.

Making Choices

As the world changes, individuals face choices about whether they should support or oppose these changes. They must decide whether to move to cities, use computers, and spray crops with insecticides. You, too, face choices about change. If there are homeless people in your community, you may urge your local government to provide housing for them. If there is air pollution where you live, you may choose to use public transportation instead of traveling by car.

Studying how people of other cultures have changed in both good and bad ways will help you make your own decisions. Learning about other cultures and regions will help you learn about yourself, your own community, and your own culture. You will also discover new things about your relationship to the rest of the world. All of these things are important in preparing you for your role in the global village of the future.

Section 3 Review

1. What are some changes that have had good and bad results?
2. **Predicting** What choices do you think you will make about your community's environment in the future?

On Assignment...

Formulating Questions: Keep a journal of questions you wrote as you read this chapter. When you find facts and examples in this book that answer your questions, write the answers in your journal. If more questions occur to you as you progress through this book, add them to your list.

CHAPTER 1

The Land and People of South and Southeast Asia

How have the land and climate affected the people of South and Southeast Asia?

Land is precious in South and Southeast Asia. Where the land is hilly, farmers cut terraces into the sides of mountains to increase the amount of land they can farm. In Bali, farmers tend their rice terraces.

Looking at Key Terms

- **subcontinent** a large landmass that juts out from a continent
- **plateau** a flat area that is higher than the land that surrounds it
- **monsoon** a seasonal wind that brings wet or dry weather
- **cyclone** a dangerous windstorm; often one that brings rain
- **delta** a triangle of land that forms where a river meets the sea
- **hydroelectricity** the power that comes from the force of rushing water
- **dialect** a regional form of a language that has its own words, expressions, and pronunciations

On Assignment...

Making a Brochure: In this chapter, you will learn about the land and people of South and Southeast Asia. Imagine that you are planning a brochure to attract tourists to this region. As you read, take notes about information that you might want to include in your brochure. Consider facts about the land, climate, and people. Look for On Assignment hint boxes. They will give you ideas about how to organize the brochure. At the end of the chapter, you will create your brochure.

SECTION 1

The Lands of South and Southeast Asia

What are the major physical features of the Indian subcontinent and of Southeast Asia?

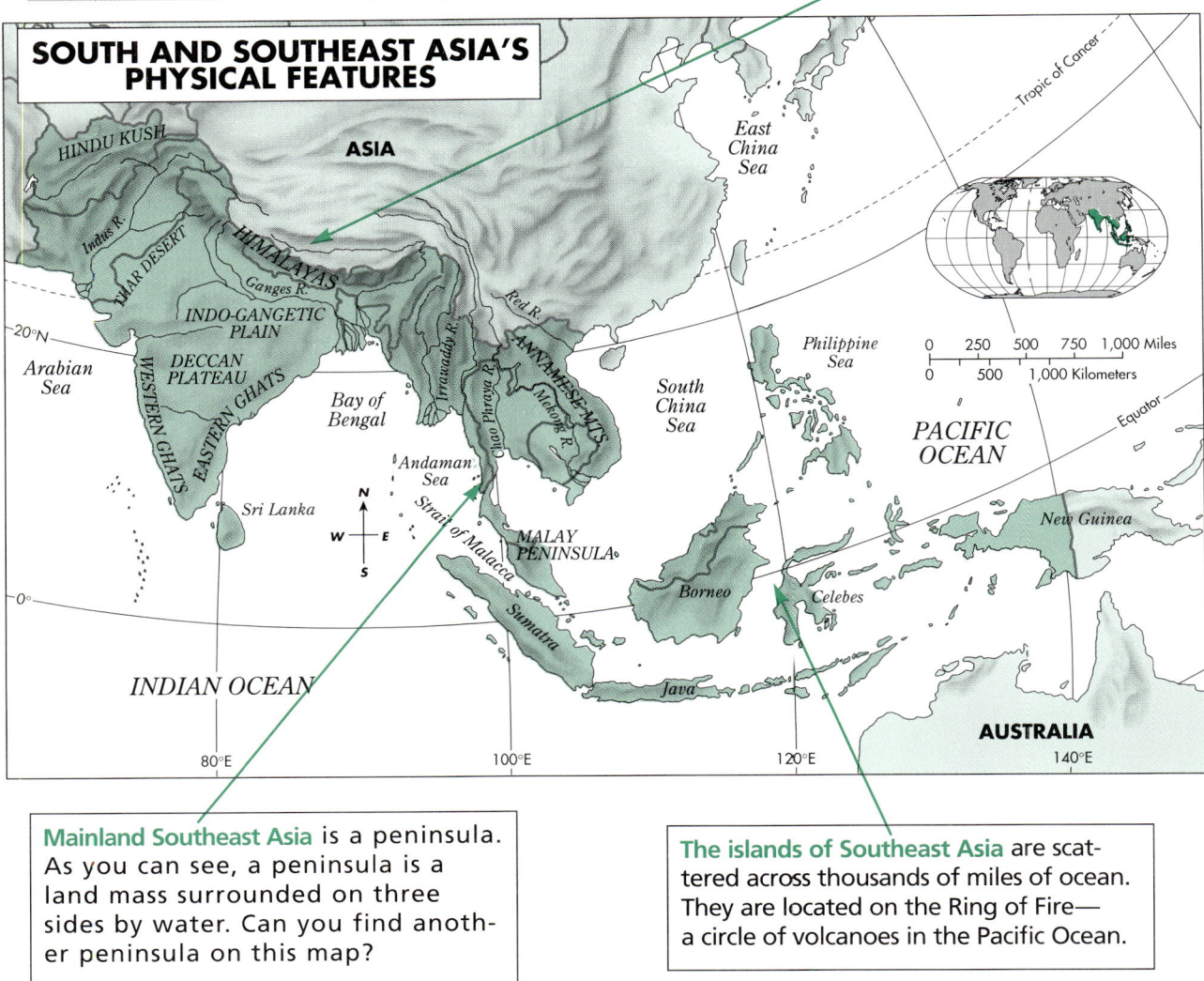

The Himalayas sweep across the north of India and into Tibet, Nepal, and Bhutan.

Mainland Southeast Asia is a peninsula. As you can see, a peninsula is a land mass surrounded on three sides by water. Can you find another peninsula on this map?

The islands of Southeast Asia are scattered across thousands of miles of ocean. They are located on the Ring of Fire—a circle of volcanoes in the Pacific Ocean.

South and Southeast Asia are located between the Indian Ocean and the Pacific Ocean. It is a region of densely populated cities, thinly populated deserts, high mountains, and fertile river valleys. Look at the map and note how the region can be divided into three subregions.

The Indian **subcontinent** is the triangle of land that juts out into the Indian Ocean. Mainland Southeast Asia is the long, thin peninsula that lies to the east of India. Island Southeast Asia is the chain of islands that stretches out into the Pacific.

THE SHAPE OF THE LAND

The Himalayas The Himalayan (him-uh-LAY-uhn) mountain range is more than 1,500 miles (2,400 km) long and 150 to 200 miles (240 to 325 km) wide. Towering 29,029 feet (8,848 m) into the sky, Mount Everest is the highest point on earth. The Himalayas are called by some "the rooftop of the world." The word *Himalaya* means "home of snow." The name fits.

A rice paddy in Southeast Asia Rice is vital to the people of Southeast Asia. For more than 5,000 years, people here have been growing rice to eat. It is the region's most common crop. In some places, it is common for farmers to raise three crops of rice a year. Thousands of years ago, farmers learned to grow rice on terraces that climb up the mountains. In this way, they made the most of the region's land.

Chapter 1　　　　　　　　　　　　　　　　　　　　　11

The Regions of the Indian Subcontinent

The Indian subcontinent can be divided into three main geographic regions. The first region is the northern mountains. These mountains form a high, steep barrier that separates India from the rest of Asia. The northern mountains slope into the northern plain. The northern plain is the second region. Low mountains divide the plain from the third region—the Deccan Plateau.

The Northern Mountains

The Hindu Kush and the Himalayas form the northern border. These high mountain ranges form a natural wall between India and the rest of Asia. Travel across these mountains is difficult. The mountains are so high that even planes have trouble flying over them.

The Himalayas and the Hindu Kush have usually kept invaders out of the subcontinent of India. However, passage through the mountains is not impossible. There are several openings through the mountains called passes. The most famous is the Khyber (KEYE•buhr) Pass. The Khyber Pass cuts through the Hindu Kush mountains.

The most important rivers of the Indian subcontinent spring from the Himalaya Mountains. The Ganges (GAN•jeez), the Indus, and the Brahmaputra (brahm•uh•POO•truh) all begin there. They are fed by the melting snow in the mountains. These rivers water the fertile lands of the northern plain.

The Northern Plain

The northern plain is located south of the northern mountains. The plain stretches for 2,000 miles (3,200 km) across Pakistan, northern India, and Bangladesh. Rivers flowing from the northern mountains bring water to the flat land of the plain. The land is made fertile by rich topsoil that river floods bring from the mountains. The region also receives abundant rainfall.

The northern plain is the most densely populated region. Almost two thirds of the region's people live there. Most of the people are farmers. Fertile land and a good climate make the northern plain one of the largest farming areas in the world.

The Indian subcontinent is bordered in the north by two mountain ranges. The Himalayas are located in the east. The Hindu Kush lie in the west. At the right, horses graze in the highlands of Kashmir.

The Thar Desert is also part of the northern plain. Located in the plain's northwest corner, this desert is 100,000 square miles (259,000 sq km) of hot, dry land.

The Deccan Plateau

The Deccan (DEK•uhn) Plateau lies to the south of the northern plain. A **plateau** is a large area of high, flat or gently rolling land. This region is shaped like a large triangle. On the northern side of the triangle lie the Vindhya (VIN•dyuh) Mountains. The Vindhyas form the boundary between northern and southern India.

Two other mountain ranges, the Eastern Ghats and Western Ghats, form the other sides of the triangle. They are called the "Ghats" for the many ghats, or passes, that cut through them. The Ghats are too high for most rain clouds to pass over. They block rain from reaching the plateau. The lack of rain makes the Deccan Plateau a dry region that is difficult to farm. The regions between the Ghats and the sea are narrow coastal plains where rain is plentiful.

The Climate of South Asia

The climate of the Indian subcontinent ranges from bitter cold to steaming hot. The high Himalayas are cold year-round, with temperatures well below freezing. In some parts of the northern plain, however, temperatures can rise to over 100° F (38° C).

In much of India and Bangladesh, there are three seasons: hot and rainy, hot and dry, or cool. In the hot and rainy season, from June to September, people expect downpours daily. During the hot, dry season, the land becomes parched. April and May are hottest. Often no rain falls for weeks.

Monsoons are a vital part of life in South Asia. **Monsoons** are winds that blow across the subcontinent. Toward the end of May, the rain-bearing monsoon begins to blow from the southwest. The wind continues to blow across the subcontinent until the end of September or October.

The winds bring about 80 percent of the region's annual rainfall. Without the rain-bearing monsoons, the land dries and there are not enough crops. When the monsoon brings the right amount of rain, there are crops to feed the subcontinent's hundreds of millions of people.

When the monsoon brings too much rain, flooding may cost thousands of lives. In 1991, a **cyclone** hit Bangladesh at the end of the summer monsoon season. About 200,000 were killed by its winds and rains. Millions were left without homes.

In October, a second monsoon season begins. The winds from the mountains of the northeast bring cool, dry air to the subcontinent.

Mountains and Climate

The mountain ranges of the subcontinent affect the climate of the region. The high mountains of the Himalayas protect India from the cold winds of Central Asia. Also, as wet winds from the Bay of Bengal hit the cold air of the Himalayas, rain falls. The rain makes the northeast portion of the subcontinent a very wet place.

Natural Resources South Asia is rich in a number of natural resources. Mineral riches include coal, iron ore, mica, gold, diamonds, sapphires, and precious woods. Nearly all of the 70 million tons of coal mined each year fuels railroads, steel plants, and other businesses. India is a major producer of iron ore.

Perhaps South Asia's greatest natural resource is its land. About three fourths of the people are farmers. Rice is grown on about a third of the farmland. Farmers grow wheat in drier areas. Tea, sugar cane, cotton, and jute (used for rope) are other important crops.

Farmers of the subcontinent once relied on traditional methods and inferior seed. In recent years, that has changed. The use of modern methods has raised food production considerably. From 1980 to 1990, food production grew by an average of 5 percent a year.

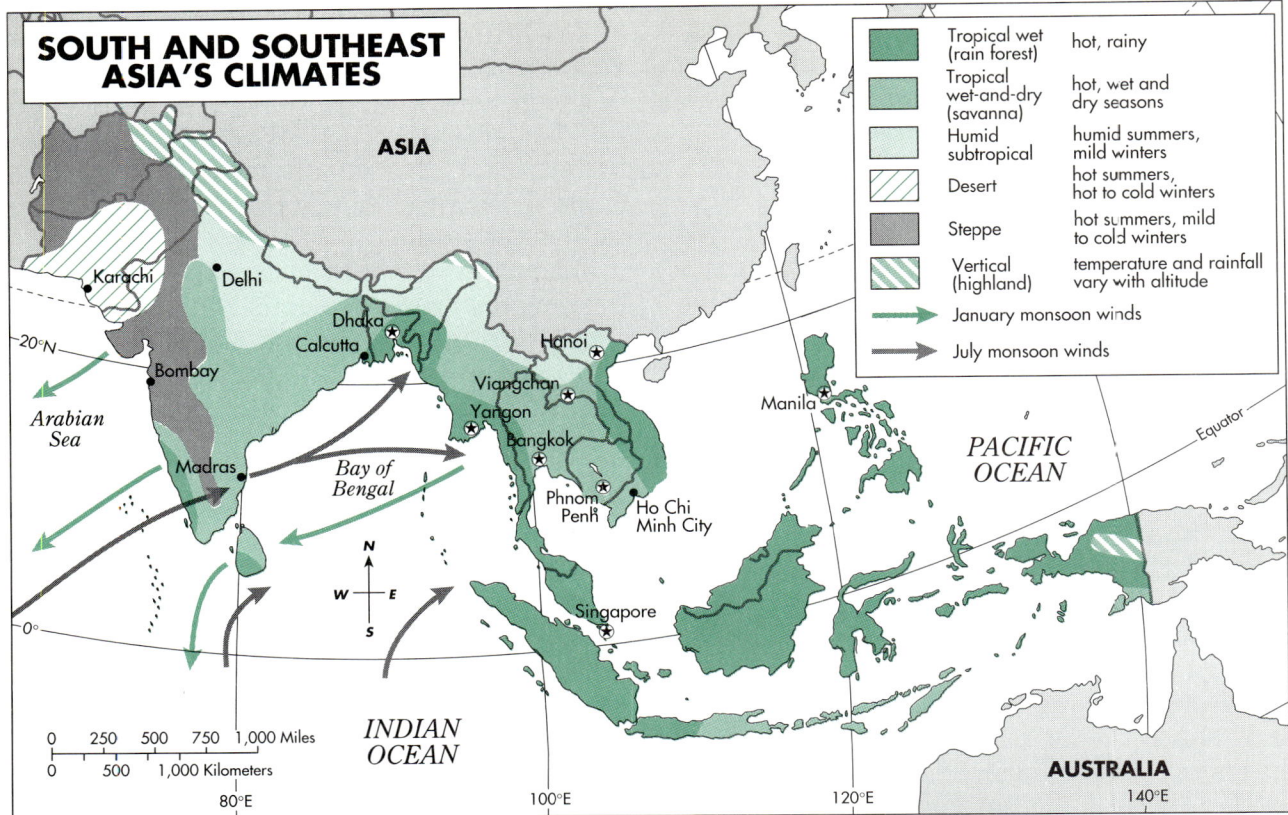

Place Much of South and Southeast Asia is affected by winds called monsoons. In which direction do the different monsoons blow? What climates are found on the islands of Southeast Asia?

Southeast Asia: Mainland and Islands

East of India is a region called Southeast Asia. Southeast Asia can be divided into two main parts: the mainland and the islands.

Mainland Southeast Asia Mainland Southeast Asia is made up of the nations of Myanmar (MEE•uhn•mahr), formerly Burma; Thailand; Laos; Cambodia; and Vietnam. These nations lie on a peninsula that juts out into the Indian Ocean and the South China Sea.

The northern portion of the region has high, rugged mountains. The steep highlands are lightly populated. The land and the climate make life difficult. Most of those who do live here occupy the flat, high plateaus. Nearly all of them make their living by farming.

Many people live in the river valleys that run through the mountains. There are four main river valleys: the Irrawaddy, Salween, Chao Phraya (CHOW•prah•YAH), and Mekong. These rivers often overflow their banks, leaving behind rich soil.

Near the shore, the rich soil that the rivers leave behind forms deltas. A **delta** is a triangle of land that forms where a river meets the sea. The land that forms in the delta is flat and the soil is good for growing crops. Most of the population of Southeast Asia lives in the delta region. The area's biggest cities are there. Yangon (Rangoon) in Myanmar, Bangkok in Thailand, and Ho Chi Mihn City (Saigon) in Vietnam are three of these cities.

Island Southeast Asia From above, the islands of Southeast Asia look like handfuls of scattered emeralds. These islands make up the largest group of islands in the world. They were formed long ago by volcanoes and by the earth's movement.

This region has the greatest number of active volcanoes in the world. It also has more earthquakes than just about anywhere. The volcanic eruptions, which spread ash and minerals, have made the soil on these islands rich. Most people on the islands live in the lowlands. For centuries, though, the islands' farmers have been building terraces into the mountains to grow rice.

Several countries make up island Southeast Asia. One is the tiny island country of Singapore. A location on a main shipping route and a good harbor have made Singapore a wealthy country.

Another small country is Brunei. It is located on the island of Borneo.

About 13,000 islands form the country of Indonesia. The Philippines, to the north, is a group of 7,107 islands. The country of Malaysia lies partly on the mainland and also in island Southeast Asia. Mountains form the backbone of the long, narrow strip of land located on the mainland. Most people live on the plains along the coasts.

The Climate of Southeast Asia

Southeast Asia is located near the equator. In general, its climate is steamy and hot. The temperature stays at about 80°F (25°C), except in the high mountains and in mainland Southeast Asia near China. There, the temperature is cooler.

Like the climate of South Asia, Southeast Asia's climate is affected by monsoons. The summer monsoons bring moisture and rain to the region. Farmers rely on the monsoon rains. When the monsoons don't bring rain, crops fail and people suffer.

Natural Resources

The land of Southeast Asia is rich in minerals. But to get to those resources, miners must be able to dig. People must be able to build roads. Many of Southeast Asia's riches are in high mountains or dense forests that are difficult to reach.

The people of Southeast Asia have developed ways to farm in the rugged mountains. There are rice paddies and tea plantations on terraced hillsides. The cool mountains are also where the region's forests grow.

Valuable teak wood comes from the tropical rain forests. Cutting the wood, however, means destroying the rain forests. The nations of Southeast Asia face the same choices as other countries with rain forests. The countries need the income that the wood brings, but they are concerned about the destruction of their environment.

Southeast Asia is the world's largest producer of tin. Indonesia is the region's largest producer of oil. When the technology improves, Southeast Asia will find ways to harvest more of its resources in iron ore, bauxite (aluminum ore), copper, nickel, gold, and precious gems.

On Assignment...

Think of what your brochure would tell tourists about the land and climate of Southeast Asia. What pictures would you want to include? What information would be helpful to tourists planning a trip?

Section 1 Review

1. Why are monsoons important to the people of South and Southeast Asia?
2. **Determining Cause and Effect** How have volcanoes affected the farmlands of Southeast Asia?

THE PEOPLE OF SOUTH AND SOUTHEAST ASIA

Hinduism is a major religion in South Asia. In India, Hinduism shapes the way of life of many people. There are more than 750 million Hindus in India, making up 83 percent of the population. To Hindus, the Ganges River is sacred, or holy. Hindus bathe in its waters to purify, or spiritually cleanse, themselves.

Muslims are followers of the religion of Islam. About 300 million Muslims live on the subcontinent of South Asia. In India, about 11 percent of the population is Muslim. Bangladesh and Pakistan are Islamic countries. In Southeast Asia, Malaysia and Indonesia are mostly Muslim countries. Islam was brought to South Asia about the year 1200 and to Southeast Asia in about 900. Islam appealed to many of the region's people because it had no caste system.

City of Angels is the Thai people's name for Bangkok, their capital and largest city. About six million people live in Bangkok. On crowded streets and waterways, people on bikes, in rickshaws, in trucks, and in boats jockey for space. They rumble past new stores and ancient sites. Some people dress in Western clothes. Others dress in traditional clothing. It is a city of skyscrapers and tar paper shacks. Like most cities of the region, Bangkok is a city of contrasts.

Peace in the Village Many Southeast Asians lead lives that are much like the lives of their parents, grandparents, and great-grandparents. Families quietly tend their rice paddies. In fact, most of Southeast Asia's people still live—and farm—in small villages. They have little land, but grow enough food for their needs.

Chapter 1   17

Case Study 1

Waiting for the Rain

The sky outside Goa was a brilliant blue. Dattu Bjupal squinted into the sun. He sighed. Around him was the brown dust of his rice fields. Without the monsoon, there would be no rice.

"Here, we say that a beautiful woman has hair black as monsoon clouds," Dattu grins. "Now, I would rather have the black clouds.

"I have faith," Dattu says. "It is June 9. The next day, maybe the next. It is time. All over India, we are waiting. In Kerala, I hear they have no power. There the water makes **hydroelectricity**. There is no water, so there is no power. But soon the rains will come."

He chuckles and explains that once the monsoon season begins, "You will find me in the rain, day after day, turning the mud into rice fields. You see this dirt? Come back in August. It will all be green. You will see rice fields like green velvet."

Dattu shades his eyes and looks out. Far in the distance, clouds gather. In nearby fields, farmers look to the sky.

"Can you smell it?" Dattu asks. "It is the smell of rain. It is coming. I know. The beautiful woman is coming."

Case Study Review

1. How do the monsoons change the land and the lives of the people in India?
2. **Predicting Consequences** What do you think will happen if the monsoon is late? What will happen if it does not come at all?

SECTION 2

The People

Who lives in South and Southeast Asia?

> **On Assignment...**
> List the information from this section that you would like to include in your brochure. Describe pictures that could illustrate your points.

Imagine that you are writing an advertisement in India. If you wanted to reach all of the people of India, you would have to translate the ad into the 16 official Indian languages, plus the 845 other languages and **dialects**. Each dialect, or regional version of a language, has its own words, expressions, and pronunciations.

You would face the same challenge in Southeast Asia. In Indonesia alone, there are 25 languages and more than 200 dialects.

The vast number of languages shows the diversity of people who live in the region. Some of the diversity has to do with the geographic features of the region. For example, the mountain ranges worked as a barrier to keep groups of people separate.

Diversity in South and Southeast Asia

The diversity of the region has many benefits. Different people have brought different ideas about government, the economy, religion, and culture. They have brought new and sometimes better ways of doing things.

But the diversity also presents great challenges. The number of different languages has created problems. When people cannot talk to one another easily, misunderstandings often occur.

The number of religions in South Asia has created problems. Islam and Hinduism have the largest numbers of followers. These two groups have clashed violently.

Within all this diversity, there are some major groupings of people. The Dravidians (druh•VIHD•ee•uhnz) live in the south of the Indian subcontinent. The Dravidians are the original inhabitants of the subcontinent. Many historians believe that the Dravidians once lived in the north. About 1500 B.C., people called the Aryans (AIR•ee• uhnz) came out of Central Asia and pushed the Dravidians south.

Southeast Asia faces many of the same problems as South Asia. Island Southeast Asia is located on a main trade route. That means that many people have passed through this region.

Sometimes the newcomers took control of the countries they settled in. For example, in Malaysia, 55 percent of the people are Islamic Malays. The others are Chinese and Indian. The Chinese-Malaysians control most of the economy. Some Malays resent this.

In most countries of Southeast Asia, there are many culture groups. As in Malaysia, one culture group often controls the economy and the government of a particular country. For example, in Laos, the Lao people make up 50 percent of the population. Other ethnic groups include the Thai, Hmong, and Yao. The Lao control the government and the best land.

The religions of Southeast Asia include Hinduism, Buddhism, Christianity, and Islam. There are many traditional religions, however. Sometimes people have blended several religions. This blending has made the cultures of Southeast Asia unique.

Section 2 Review

1. Why is there so much diversity among the people of South and Southeast Asia?
2. **Drawing Conclusions** What challenges are created when a country has more than one or two official languages?

REVIEWING CHAPTER 1

I. Reviewing Vocabulary
Match each word on the left with the correct definition on the right.

1. cyclone
2. hydroelectricity
3. monsoon
4. plateau

a. a seasonal wind that brings wet or dry weather
b. a flat area that is higher than the land that surrounds it
c. a dangerous windstorm; often one that brings rain
d. the power that comes from the force of rushing water

II. Understanding the Chapter
Answer the questions below on a separate sheet of paper.

1. How do mountains affect India's climate?
2. Identify three important rivers in India. From where do these rivers flow?
3. How has the location of Island Southeast Asia contributed to the diversity of the region's population?
4. How have immigrants from China and India influenced Malaysia?

III. Building Skills: Identifying Cause and Effect
In each of the pairs below, identify the cause or the effect.

1. Effect: The Deccan Plateau gets little rain. What is the cause?
2. Cause: Many of the natural resources of Southeast Asia are found in steep mountains or under dense forests. What is the effect?
3. Cause: The mountain ranges in South Asia keep people separated. What is the effect?

IV. Working Together
Work with a group to create quiz questions and answers about the land and people of South and Southeast Asia. Take turns with the other groups asking and answering the questions.

On Assignment...

Making a Brochure: Study the notes that you took for your brochure about the land and the people of South and Southeast Asia. You will create a four-page brochure about the land and the people of the region. First, decide how you want to organize the information. Next, sketch the brochure deciding where you will place the pictures. Then, write the copy. Now put the pictures and copy together to create an attractive, informative brochure.

CHAPTER 2

The History of South Asia

What were the major historical developments in South Asia from early civilizations to independence?

To honor his wife, Shah Jahan built the Taj Mahal in Agra, India. Workers began the building in 1631 and finished it in 1648. The massive dome is made of white marble and inlaid gems.

Looking at Key Terms

- **descendant** a person who can trace his or her heritage to an individual or group
- **caste** a social group based on birth; the system that separates Hindus by class and job
- **meditate** to think deeply
- **reincarnated** reborn
- **nirvana** a state in which a person has achieved perfect happiness because he or she wants nothing
- **mosque** a place of worship for Muslims
- **civil disobedience** a person's refusal to follow laws that he or she believes are unjust

On Assignment...

Creating a Mural: By creating a mural, you can put what you learn into picture form. In each section of this chapter, you will make notes about the most important events that occurred on the subcontinent. You will also make sketches of what you want in your mural. At the end of the chapter, you will make a sketch of your mural. Then you will complete it.

SECTION 1

An Ancient Heritage: Early Civilizations of India

What were some of the early civilizations and empires of South Asia?

The scientist rubbed her hand over a small clay figure. She looked out over the Indus valley. Workers were uncovering houses and roads that had been buried for thousands of years. The scientist tried to imagine what life was like in the valley in 1500 B.C. At that time, the Indus people had been living there peacefully for 1,000 years. They had water and sewer systems, sturdy houses, and public baths. The people of the Indus were farmers and traders. They may even have been the first to weave cotton. What the Indus people didn't know, the woman thought, was that their civilization would soon come to an end.

The Aryans In about 1500 B.C., invaders arrived from the north. These invaders were the Aryans. The Aryans marched through the mountain passes in the Hindu Kush. Over the next few hundred years, waves of Aryans continued to come. Some scientists believe that the Aryan invasion contributed to the decline of Indus valley civilization. The people of the Indus valley moved south. Many historians believe that their **descendants** are the Dravidians, who live in the south of India today.

From religious writings called the Vedas (VAY•duhz), we know about the Aryans. The Vedas were written in Sanskrit, the written language developed by the Aryans. The Vedas describe the Aryans' love of war, horse-drawn chariots, music, and dance.

The Vedas also tell about Aryan religious beliefs. For example, the Aryans worshipped many gods, including Indra, Varuna, Vishnu, Siva, and Devi. They believed that the souls of people are reborn after they die.

The Aryan Caste System Another important part of Aryan society was the **caste** system. A caste is a social group based on birth. All people in Aryan society were divided into groups. At the top of the caste system were the kings and nobles. Next were the priests, or Brahmans. Third were ordinary tribesmen and herders. Fourth were the people whom the Aryans had conquered. At the bottom were the Untouchables, or the outcastes. The Untouchables did the dirty work of society. Later the order of the first and second castes switched. The priests became the first caste and the kings and nobles became the second caste.

A part of the caste system were the ideas of karma and dharma. *Karma* means "fate." According to Hindu beliefs, people who do good deeds throughout their lives can earn good karma. This allows them to be reborn into a higher caste in their next lives.

People who are evil achieve bad karma. They are punished by being reborn into a lower caste. Part of attaining good karma is to follow one's *dharma*, or duty. If Hindus follow the dharma of their caste, they earn a higher caste in the next life.

As time went on, the Aryan caste system became stricter and more complex. The caste system then became an important part of Hinduism, which is the main religion of India today.

Religion in South Asia

Hinduism and Buddhism, two world religions, developed in South Asia. Islam is a third religion that is important in the region today. Islam developed in the Middle East and spread to South Asia.

Hinduism Hinduism is one of the oldest religions in the world. It has no known founder and no formal church. It developed from ancient Aryan culture and traditions. Hinduism is a system of living more than a set of beliefs. Most Hindus chant a prayer to the sun at dawn. Aside from that, there are few prayers that all Hindus say. Most

The founder of Buddhism was Siddhartha Gautama, who was an Indian prince. Siddhartha believed that people would find peace if they did good deeds and lived a good life. Shown here is a Buddhist temple in Java, Indonesia.

worship Siva, Vishnu, or Devi. They may also worship gods that are special to their town or their family.

Hinduism does not have a bible, or holy book. There are, however, sacred, or holy, Hindu texts. Among these are the Vedas and the Upanishads (oo•PAN•ih•shadz). Most Hindus are familiar with the *Mahabharata* (muh•HAH•bah•rah•tuh). The *Mahabharata*, which means "The Great Story" in Sanskrit, is a very long poem that tells the story of a 12-year war between two branches of a royal family.

The most famous section of the *Mahabharata* is the *Bhagavad-Gita* (BAHG•uh•vuhd GEE•tah). It tells of a soldier who meets the god Krishna on the eve of an important battle. Krishna advises the warrior to **meditate**, or think deeply; to do good works; and to love God. Krishna also tells him to do his duty as a soldier. In the end, the soldier is victorious.

Most Hindus do not eat meat. Hindus also believe in the caste system. They believe that people are born to their job and their status in life. If a person does his or her job well, he or she will be **reincarnated**, or reborn, into a higher caste.

Caste still rules Indian life today. The caste system divides people into classes and restricts them from certain jobs. It has been a barrier to civil rights in India. People who believe in the caste system think that sons should have the same job as their fathers and that a person in one caste may not marry a person from another caste. People in the lowest castes are often treated poorly. In the 1950s and 1960s, India's government passed laws that bar discrimination against any caste for any reason. But the laws are hard to enforce. Especially in the rural areas of India, the caste system remains strong. (See Chapter 3.)

Buddhism Buddhism is another religion that began in South Asia. It was begun in India during the 500s B.C. by a man named Siddhartha Gautama (sid•DAHRT•uh gow•TAH•muh). Siddhartha was born a prince in what is now the country of Nepal.

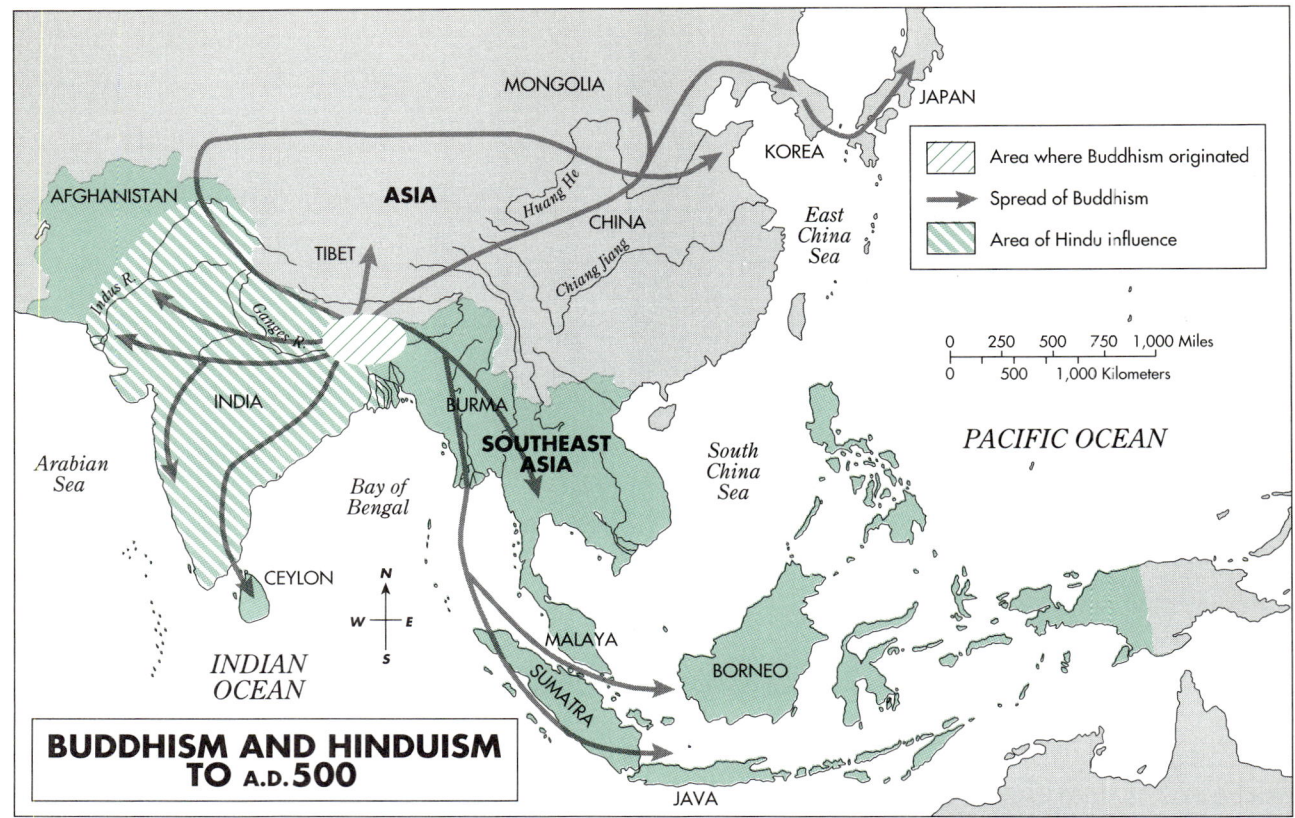

Movement and Region Buddhism and Hinduism both began in South Asia. From there, the two religions spread. To which countries did Buddhism spread?

When he was about 30, he wandered outside of the palace and saw four things that changed his life: an old man, a sick man, a dead man, and a contented beggar. It was the first time in his life that he had seen misery. Suddenly, he realized that life is full of suffering and pain.

Siddhartha could not rest until he found the reasons for this pain and suffering. He left his wife and newborn son and wandered for six years. He looked for answers everywhere. He began to meditate. For 49 days, he sat under a tree. Then, one day the answers suddenly came to him. At that moment, Siddhartha experienced enlightenment. From then on he was known as *Buddha,* which means "Enlightened One." Buddha called the ideas that had come to him the Four Noble Truths. They are:

- Life is full of pain and suffering.
- Desire, or wanting things, causes this pain.
- The way to end pain is to end desire.
- One can learn to end desire.

Buddha believed that if people lost their desire for possessions, they would be happy. When people did good deeds and lived a good life, they would reach **nirvana** (nihr•VAH•nuh). Nirvana is a state in which a person wants nothing.

Buddha spent the rest of his life teaching his beliefs. His followers spread Buddha's teachings far and wide. Over the next thousand years, Buddhism spread throughout Asia. (See the map above.) In India, though, many of Buddha's beliefs became part of Hinduism. Today, fewer than 1 percent of the people of India are Buddhists. Although there are only 6.4 million Buddhists in India, there are about 330 million in the world.

Today, there are two main groups of Buddhists. Theravada (ther•uh•VAH•duh) Buddhists stress a solitary life as the way to reach nirvana. They believe that Buddha was a great teacher, but not a god. Mahayana (mah•huh•YAH•nuh) Buddhists believe that Buddha was a god and they worship him.

Islam The religion of Islam is important in South Asia. Islam began during the A.D. 600s in the Middle East. It first came to South Asia in the 700s. Later, in the 1200s, more people of the subcontinent converted to Islam. Followers of Islam call themselves Muslims. There are about 230 million Muslims in Pakistan and Bangladesh. In India, there are about 128 million Muslims.

Muhammad founded Islam. Muhammad, who lived in Saudi Arabia, taught that there is one God. He preached against worshipping many gods and emphasized that all people are equal before Allah. *Allah* is the Arabic word for God. Muhammad said that for Muslims to gain Allah's grace, they must obey Allah's will. In fact, the word *Islam* means "submission to Allah."

The Koran is the holy book of Islam. Muslims believe that the Koran contains the word of God. The Koran is the basis for law all over the Muslim world.

For Muslims, there are five main duties. They are known as the Five Pillars of Islam. The most important pillar is the belief in one God. The second is prayer. Muslims must pray five times a day. When they pray, they face Mecca, the birthplace of Muhammad.

Islam teaches concern for the poor. Giving charity is the third pillar. The fourth is fasting. During the holy month of Ramadan, Muslims fast during the day. At night, they feast. The fifth pillar is a pilgrimage to Mecca, the holy city in Saudi Arabia. Once in every Muslim's life, he or she is expected to go to Mecca.

The Golden Temple in Amritsar, India, is the Sikh religion's most important holy site. Built in 1604, the temple lies on an island connected to the mainland by a causeway.

Islam emphasizes that all believers are equal before God. This idea appealed to many Hindus who were trapped in low castes. From the 1200s to the 1500s, thousands in the northern regions of the Indian subcontinent converted to Islam.

Other Religions Other religions are also found in South Asia. They include Jainism (JEYEN•ihz•um), Sikhism (SEEK•ihz•um), and Christianity. Jainism began in the 500s B.C. as a reaction against Hinduism. Its followers promise to kill no living thing, to tell no lies, and to steal nothing. Jainists are strict vegetarians. Vegetarians do not eat meat. Today, there are more than three million Jains. Most live in western India.

Chapter 2

The Sikh religion was founded by a Hindu teacher in the 1400s. Sikhs believe in one God and do not believe in the caste system. They do believe in reincarnation. Sikhs do not cut their hair, and Sikh men usually wear turbans. They do not use tobacco or alcohol. Most of the region's more than 18 million Sikhs live in the Punjab. The Punjab is located in the northwestern portion of the subcontinent.

Christian missionaries first arrived in India in the 1500s. Through the centuries, a number of Indians have converted to Christianity. Today, there are more than 22 million Christians in India.

The Empires of India

The first of South Asia's great empires was the Maurya (MAWR•yah) Empire, which was formed in about 321 B.C. by Chandragupta (chuhn•druh•GUP•tuh) Maurya. Chandragupta was king of a small northeastern region of the subcontinent. In the 300s B.C., he took over kingdoms to the north and west. Before long, the Maurya empire reached from Afghanistan in the west to the Ganges River in the east. At its height, the Maurya empire extended over all but the most southern portion of India.

The Maurya Empire The Maurya Empire had a well-organized government. Its many government officials owed their jobs to the emperor. There was also a secret police force that sent reports to Chandragupta. The secret police warned the emperor about plots against him. A huge army of 700,000 soldiers, 9,000 elephants, and 10,000 chariots helped Chandragupta maintain order.

Chandragupta worked to improve business and trade for his people. The emperor built canals to bring water to farms. He constructed roads to transport goods to market. Ships from the Maurya Empire traded with the Middle East and other parts of Asia.

The most famous Maurya emperor was Chandragupta's grandson Asoka. Asoka ruled from 273 to 232 B.C. At first, he fought to make the empire larger. In the wars that Asoka waged, more than 100,000 people died. When Asoka learned about the deaths, he was horrified. He decided to give up war and to rule through kindness and peace. Asoka became a Buddhist.

As a Buddhist, Asoka tried to rule by his good example, rather than by the use of force. He built hospitals, rest houses for travelers, and wells to provide water for people to drink. Asoka sent teachers all over the empire to educate his subjects. To inspire people to do good works, Asoka carved messages of kindness on rocks and in caves throughout the empire. One message asked people to treat one another kindly and fairly.

India's Golden Age After the death of Asoka, the Maurya Empire declined. The empire split into many small kingdoms. It was not until the A.D. 300s that the next great empire arose. This was the Gupta Empire. The Gupta Empire lasted from 320 to 535.

Under the Guptas, science, mathematics, art, and literature flourished. It was during this period, called India's golden age, that Indian mathematicians developed the idea of zero. Doctors performed plastic surgery. Buildings were filled with sculptures. Poets wrote stirring works.

A Chinese Buddhist monk who traveled in India between 401 and 410 recorded what he saw in the Gupta Empire. The monk noted that the people of the empire "were prosperous and happy," and that the emperor was a fair man who punished criminals according to the seriousness of their crime. For example, the monk wrote, "even for a second attempt at rebellion the punishment is only the loss of the right hand."

Ancient India's golden age ended when invaders from Central Asia swept through the northern mountains. The Gupta Empire broke apart. For the next 1,000 years, India was divided into small warring kingdoms.

Islam in South Asia The next force to unify India was Islam. In about 1200, Islamic rulers set up a kingdom in northern

India. This kingdom, including the city of Delhi and the area around it, became known as the Delhi sultanate. It became famous as a center of Islam.

Mongols from Central Asia invaded and weakened the Delhi sultanate in 1398. In 1526, another Mongol invasion delivered the final blow to the sultanate. The invaders established the Mogul Empire. (*Mogul* is the Persian word for "Mongol." The Persians were part of the invading army.) Babur, who headed this army, became its first emperor.

Babur did not respect the Hindus. Islam, he believed, was the greatest religion. Under Babur's rule, Hindus paid heavy taxes and could not hold government jobs. Hindu temples were destroyed and looted.

Babur's grandson Akbar felt differently about Hindus. Akbar became emperor in 1556. He felt that it would be impossible to keep his empire united if he tried to make all the people live as Muslims. Akbar decided to allow people of all religions to worship as they pleased. Akbar believed that "If men walk in the way of God's will, interference with them would be unfair."

The Mogul Empire lasted for more than 300 years. Under the Moguls, great monuments, palaces, and **mosques**, or Muslim houses of worship, were built in India. The greatest of these buildings was the Taj Mahal, which was built as a monument to the wife of a Mogul emperor.

India became one of the richest countries in the world. Mogul rule extended over all but a small part of southern India.

Eventually, weak rulers had trouble keeping the empire together. In the 1700s, civil wars and revolts caused the empire to collapse.

Section 1 Review

1. What are the Five Pillars of Islam?
2. **Inferring** How do you think Akbar's religious tolerance kept his empire unified?

SECTION 2

Europeans Arrive

How did Britain gain control of India?

Europeans had been trading with India for hundreds of years. They valued India's spices, tea, jewels, silks, and cotton. For most of those years, Italy controlled the trade routes to India. Then, in 1498, Portuguese explorers discovered an all-sea route to India that cut Italy out of the trade. Soon after, the Portuguese built trading posts in India. Other European nations followed. All competed for the control of trade with India, but by the 1700s, only Britain and France remained.

Britain and France fought a long and bitter struggle for the control of India. By the 1760s, however, the British had defeated the French and won control. The British controlled trade through the British East India Company. The East India Company was owned by a group of British business people who traded in Indian spices, silks, and dyes. The company used the decline of the Mogul Empire to gain power. As the Mogul Empire declined, India broke apart into rival kingdoms. The British encouraged rivalry between the kingdoms and forced one Indian ruler after another to sign treaties. The treaties gave the East India Company a great deal of power.

On Assignment...

What parts of this section would you show on your mural? How might you show the religions of South Asia? How might you portray the differences between Babur and Akbar?

Chapter 2

The Sepoy Rebellion (1857–1859) was a turning point in British rule over India. After the rebellion, the British decided to increase their control over the subcontinent.

The Sepoy Rebellion By the mid-1800s, the East India Company controlled most of north India. It created an army of Indian soldiers, called *sepoys*. The company also made other changes. It made English the official language of India and required Indian schools to teach European history, literature, and science. British missionaries were allowed to convert Indians to Christianity.

Indians saw their culture, language, and religious beliefs threatened by these outsiders. The final straw came when rumors spread among the sepoys that rifle cartridges had been greased with beef fat or pork fat. To use their rifles, the sepoys had to bite off part of the cartridge. Hindus believe that bulls are sacred and Muslims do not eat pork. Both groups felt that the British had insulted them and their religious beliefs. In 1857, a revolt broke out. The sepoys nearly defeated the British. In the end, however, the British crushed the revolt.

After the Sepoy Rebellion, the British government decided to end the rule of the East India Company. India had become Britain's most important colony. Britain, therefore, decided to rule it directly.

Under the new arrangement, India was divided. The British ruled about three fifths of the subcontinent directly. The rest was run by Indians, but under British control. Indians had little or nothing to say about how they were ruled.

Effects of British Rule

The chief goal of the British government in India was to help British business. The government encouraged India's farmers to grow more cotton for Britain's new cloth-making factories. Indians were not allowed to weave their own cotton into cloth or import machinery to make cloth. For hundreds of years, weaving cotton had been the way many Indian families earned their living. Now many families had no work.

At the same time, another problem arose. Many farmers who planted cotton stopped growing food crops. This resulted in a reduced amount of food available for India's fast-growing population. Low food supplies caused hunger and starvation in much of India in the late 1800s.

The British made some changes in India that improved the lives of the Indian people. Some changes helped Britain rule India more efficiently. For example, the British dammed rivers and built canals to bring water to farmlands and to grow more crops. The British built many railroads to help move food and supplies to all parts of the country. These railroads—together with new telegraph lines—helped to tie the country together. In addition, the British ended wars between the rulers of the Indian states and prevented many conflicts between Hindus and Muslims. They brought the many different peoples of India under the authority of one government.

The British also introduced changes in education and in the legal system that benefited the Indian people. The British started many schools and universities. The students in these schools learned Western ideas about freedom and democracy. It was this group of educated people that would lead the movement for freedom for India and fight for their rights in the courts.

Section 2 Review

1. How did the British East India Company take control of India?
2. **Drawing Conclusions** The British called the sepoy uprising the Sepoy Rebellion. Indians called it the First War of Indian Independence. Why do you think they had different names for it?

SECTION 3

India Wins Independence

How did India win independence from Britain?

The Indian National Congress (INC) was formed in 1885 to fight for Indians' rights. At first, it simply wanted more Indians in government. Gradually, however, the INC began to make more demands.

During World War I, Indians backed Britain with money and soldiers. More than a million Indians served in the war. Afterwards, Indians pressured Britain for more reforms. In the city of Amritsar, protests broke out and British soldiers killed almost 400 unarmed Indians and wounded 1,200.

The British government refused to punish the soldiers for firing into an unarmed crowd. The INC, however, held its own investigation, which was led by Mohandas K. Gandhi (MOH•han•dahs GAHN•dee). Gandhi was a British-educated Hindu. In 1920, Gandhi became the leader of the INC. He wanted India to achieve independence through nonviolent means.

Gandhi Urges Nonviolence

Gandhi believed in **civil disobedience**, or a person's refusal to follow laws that he or she believes are unjust. He urged Indians to refuse to pay taxes, serve in the government, and obey British laws.

The British imprisoned Gandhi for two years for breaking the law. There he went on hunger strikes to protest British rule. After his release, Gandhi's reputation grew. He became known as *Mahatma*, which means "great soul."

Gandhi continued to encourage a program of noncooperation. He also called on Indians to appreciate their own culture. He told them, "Don't pay your taxes or send your children to an English-supported school. Send them to a school where they may learn their own native language. Make your own cotton cloth by spinning the thread at home, and don't buy English-made goods." Gandhi himself wore a homespun loincloth and became a strict vegetarian. His spinning wheel became an important symbol of protest against British domination.

The British granted more self-government to India. However, Gandhi and the INC decided that India must be completely independent. When World War II broke out in 1939, Gandhi urged the Indian people not to take part unless the British granted India

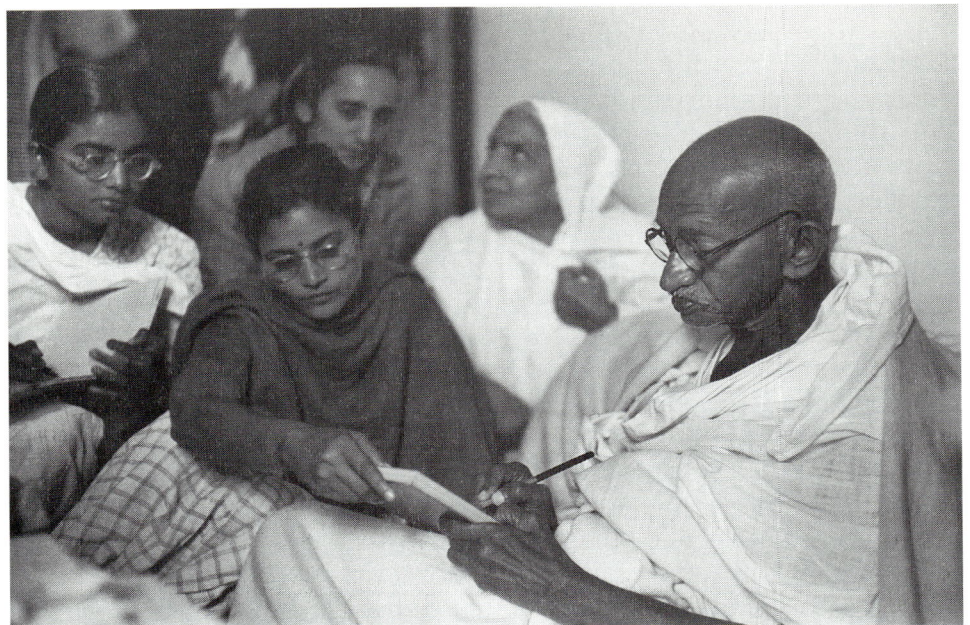

Mohandas K. Gandhi believed in the use of civil disobedience and other nonviolent methods to achieve Indian independence. Many people called him *Mahatama*, which means "great soul."

full independence. In 1942, Gandhi and other INC leaders were jailed again. Even so, more than two million Indians fought for Britain.

The end of World War II meant the end of many European empires. The British were ready to let go. The question was whether India should be one country or two. Many Muslims wanted a separate country. They felt that they could not live with the Hindus. Gandhi felt strongly that India should be united.

India Divided

In 1947, Britain granted India independence. There would be two countries. One, Pakistan, would be the home of most Muslims.

Gandhi refused to attend the Independence Day celebration. He hated the idea of India being split. As soon as the plan was decided, Hindus began to leave Pakistan. Muslims fled to Pakistan. During these flights, there were fights that killed more than a half-million people.

Gandhi began a fast to the death to stop the violence. When leaders of the groups promised to end the fighting, he ended his fast. Even so, there was more killing. In 1948, a Hindu shot and killed Gandhi. The killer was angry that Gandhi was trying to make peace with the Muslims.

Gandhi's teachings inspired many people. In the United States, he inspired civil rights leader Martin Luther King, Jr. The startling idea that one could use peace to fight war had taken hold in the world.

On Assignment...

List the events or people from this section that would be most important to include in your mural. Then write how you could illustrate them. Make rough sketches of your ideas.

Section 3 Review

1. Why did India split into two countries after it gained independence?
2. **Hypothesizing** Why do you think Gandhi was so successful?

Case Study 2

Salt March for Freedom

Prem and his friend Ram looked down the dusty road. People began to gather on the road to watch the group coming toward them.

"I know who it is," said a woman. "It is Gandhi."

"Gandhi?" The news flew like wildfire around the village.

As the man came closer, Prem could see that it was Gandhi. That kindly face, the glasses, the bald head. Near Gandhi, a man was talking. "We are walking to the sea," he was saying. "We will not pay for British salt. We will make our own. They cannot tax that. We must prove that we do not need the British. We must prove that we want our freedom. This will do that. Will you come with us?"

Prem watched as people in the village looked at one another. Some talked. Some went to their houses and came out with bundles to take with them on the trip to the sea.

"How far is it?" called out one man. "How long?"

"We have been walking for four days," a man called back. "It is about 200 miles (320 km) to the sea. We will be there in 20 days."

Ram said to Prem, "I will go to spend this time with Gandhi and to prove that the British cannot beat us down."

In an instant, Prem made up his mind. "I will go, too."

They and several other villagers left with Gandhi. The days were long, hot, and dusty. There was little food. At night, the people slept on the road. But as the group moved on, it grew. As it grew, a sense of joy filled the thousands on the road. The slight man wearing the simple white loincloth could do that. At night, he talked to the crowds. He spoke of peace and of the rightness of the cause.

At the sea, Ram, Prem and thousands of others followed Gandhi to the salt water. They set it in dishes to let the water evaporate. The police were waiting. Gandhi went with them quietly. A light shone in his eyes as he looked to his followers. He smiled.

"Do you know," Ram said, "I do believe we will succeed."

Case Study Review

1. What did Gandhi intend to prove with the Salt March?
2. **Drawing Conclusions** Why do you think people followed Gandhi to the sea?

REVIEWING CHAPTER 2

I. Reviewing Vocabulary
Match each word on the left with the correct definition on the right.

1. caste
2. meditate
3. reincarnated
4. mosque

a. a place of worship for Muslims
b. a social group based on birth
c. to think deeply
d. reborn

II. Understanding the Chapter
Answer the questions below on a separate sheet of paper.

1. How did Aryan culture lead to the development of the Hindu religion?
2. What are the major religions of South Asia?
3. What were the causes of the sepoy uprising?
4. What were the original goals of the Indian National Congress? How did those goals change?

III. Building Skills: Identifying a Point of View
Look at each of the statements below. Then match each statement with the person or group who might have had this point of view.

1. a Buddhist
2. Gandhi
3. a British officer
4. a Muslim

a. We will succeed if we oppose the government without violence.
b. The prophet Muhammad heard the voice of God.
c. If you stop wanting things, you will be happy.
d. We have improved this country with roads, railroads, and schools.

IV. Working Together
Work with two or three classmates to create a time line that shows major events in the history of South Asia. First, review the chapter and list all of these events. Then, arrange them in chronological, or time, order. Finally, transfer your time line to a large sheet of paper and place it on the bulletin board to use as a classroom reference.

On Assignment...
Creating a Mural: Look at the notes and sketches that you made throughout this chapter. Think of how the pictures could tell a story from beginning to end. Now create your mural.

CHAPTER 3

Changing Patterns of Life in South Asia

How and why are traditions changing in South Asia?

In India, as elsewhere in the world, education is the key to success. These children attend a school in Gujarat, India, which has a satellite TV dish.

Looking at Key Terms

- **epidemic** an outbreak of disease
- **bustee** a poor area of a city where people live in shacks
- **stupa** a dome-shaped burial mound that serves as a Buddhist holy site
- **raga** one of the ancient melody patterns of Indian music
- **epic** a long poem that tells the story of a hero

On Assignment...

Writing Letters: Imagine that you are traveling throughout South Asia. Your assignment is to write letters home that describe the people you meet and the way they live. In your letters, you may wish to compare the way of life in South Asia to the way of life in the United States. Take notes as you read and look for hint boxes to help you write your letters. At the end of the section, you will review your notes and write one letter to your family and another to a friend about what you have observed.

SECTION 1

India: A Land of Tradition and Change

What changes have occurred in India since independence?

"How long since you have been home?" asks Keval. He is on the dirt street of his village to the north of New Delhi. "A decade? Two? Come in! Sit down! Let me tell you how life has changed. It has changed all over India." Keval ticks off with his fingers. "First, the caste system is changed. Second, life in our village is so different. Most of my sons are gone. And, last, I must tell you about the women. The women in India–well, you would not know them."

Keval settles in on a mat in the small mud-brick house. Most of the people in his village are farmers. "I have not decided how I feel about all these changes. Many in our village do not like it. But still—" Keval's arm sweeps the village outside. "Still people move from here. They go to the cities. There, the changes are really something. You know, in the cities, caste does not matter so much. Sons work at different jobs than their fathers. They marry women who are not in their caste.

"Some people from the village have moved to the cities. They go to school and get an education. Then most of them do not want to follow the caste traditions. The law, too, says that everyone can vote now. Before, that was not the case. Did you hear what happened in 1990? Government jobs—27 percent—were set aside for Untouchables. Students in the cities set fire to themselves in protest. Feelings run strong, my friend."

Village Life and City Life

"Here in the village, life is different for those who stay behind. There is not enough land for everyone. My sons have left. They cannot be farmers as I am. They are in the city, learning a trade. Then," Keval shrugs, "they may be back. Or maybe not. It is sure they will not be farmers. But life is better in the village now. We have electricity. We have a hospital."

Keval stops as a young woman comes in the door. She smiles fondly at him. "Do you remember my daughter, Geeta?" Keval asks the question with pride. Geeta turns her

COUNTRIES OF SOUTH ASIA

COUNTRY	CAPITAL CITY	AREA (square miles)	POPULATION (millions of people)	POPULATION DOUBLING TIME (years)
Bangladesh	Dhaka	50,260	113.9	29
Bhutan	Thimphu	18,150	1.4	30
India	New Delhi	1,147,950	897.4	34
Maldives	Malé	120	0.2	20
Nepal	Kathmandu	52,820	20.4	28
Pakistan	Islamabad	297,640	122.4	23
Sri Lanka	Colombo	24,950	17.8	49

Source: World Population Data Sheet of the Population Reference Bureau, Inc.

The populations of the countries of South Asia are growing quickly. In how many years will the population of India double? Which country's population is due to double fastest?

Today, women in India have more opportunity than ever before to attend universities and to work outside the home. The women in this picture are nuns who work in the laboratory of a Christian mission hospital in Mahuadanr, Bihar.

large brown eyes to the visitor. She is wearing a printed cotton skirt and a white shirt. "We are looking for a husband for Geeta. She will marry someone from here, I hope. Then she will stay here. In some parts of India, women go to college. Not from this village, though. Geeta will marry a man we choose for her. And if later, they love each other. . . ." Keval shrugs.

"Father," says Geeta. "That is not so, what you said. Just last year, Saroj went to university. She will become a nurse. And now women can vote. We can buy land and sell it. All that is in the last few decades. Do not forget Indira Gandhi. She ran the whole of India. And doctors—India has more women doctors than the United States!"

Keval sighs. Then he strokes his daughter's hand. "Yes, yes," he says. "Some women do these things. But in this village, the role of wife is still most important. And do not worry. We will find you a good husband."

Geeta looks at her father and smiles. "Yes, father," she says. "But do not be surprised if we live in a different way."

"You see?" Keval says, laughing. "You asked what has changed. Listen to how this daughter speaks to her father!"

Section 1 Review

1. Why do people from the villages move to the cities?
2. **Summarizing** Explain the main changes that have come to Keval's village.

SECTION 2

India: Future Trends

What challenges will India face in the future?

India is the second most populous country in the world. It ranks second only to China. From 1965 to 1985, the population in India rose more than 60 percent.

To think about what that means, consider this. The United States had 248 million people in 1990, while India had 911 million. There are about 70 people per square mile in the United States. In India, there are 741

On Assignment...

Imagine that you have been the visitor in Keval and Geeta's home. What would you tell the people at home about the changes in India?

Chapter 3

35

people per square mile. That means that India has 10 times as many people per square mile as does the United States.

A Growing Population

One reason India is growing so fast is that the death rate is down. Today, fewer people die from **epidemics**, or outbreaks of disease. Epidemics of smallpox and malaria used to kill many Indians.

India's government is trying to slow the growth of the population. At first, some states fined couples who had more than two children. Now, the government is trying to convince couples to have fewer children instead of punishing those who have many children. No one knows if this voluntary family planning will work.

Overpopulation has caused some serious problems in India. It is difficult to provide food, housing, jobs, and medical care for so many people. But population is only one of India's concerns.

Saving the Environment

The environment is another cause for concern. Many trees have been cut down in India's highland. When an area is cleared of trees, there is nothing to hold the soil in place. When the rains come, the soil simply washes away.

People in the highlands use a form of civil disobedience to stop loggers from cutting more trees. The people simply hug the trees. To cut down the trees, the loggers would have to hurt the tree huggers. Others around the world have used this idea to save trees.

South Asia faces other environmental problems as well. Overuse of farmland is one. Unsafe water and sewage in the cities is another. Air pollution is a big problem, too. In 1984, the name Bhopal became known to the whole world. That was the year that a leak at a chemical plant caused at least 1,500 people to die.

The Indian government has worked hard to deal with all these problems. The solutions may be years away, though.

The Move to the Cities

Most people still live in villages in India. However, farmland is becoming scarce. Many people move to the cities to find jobs. Often, that does not happen. The cities are overcrowded. In Bombay, for example, more than one million people live in **bustees**, or poor areas filled with shacks. Bombay's bustees form some of the largest shantytowns in the world. There are a half-million people who cannot even manage to live in a bustee. Those people sleep on the streets.

On a crowded street in Bombay, India, car horns blow as traffic backs up. With more than 12 million people, Bombay is India's most populous city. Like most cities, Bombay is a city of contrasts in wealth and poverty.

Bombay is not the only city in South Asia with bustees. Bustees exist in other Indian cities as well as in Kathmandu, Nepal; and Karachi, Pakistan. One of the main problems is that there are simply not enough jobs. People without jobs cannot afford housing of any sort. They live in the bustees, where cardboard or rags can make the walls of a home. Safe drinking water and public toilets are sometimes hard to find. City officials are trying to keep up with the new city dwellers and their needs, but it is hard. People keep pouring into the cities.

For the wealthy, living in a city can be good. The wealthy have large apartments. There are private schools and servants. People come to their doors to sell food. India's large middle class also finds opportunities in the cities. The cities provide access to a wide range of jobs and to schooling.

Education in India

Although wealthy and middle-class city dwellers are likely to be educated, only 43 percent of India's people can read and write. Because most high-paying jobs require literacy skills, people who cannot read and write have difficulty improving their lives. India has pledged that every child will have a free education to the age of 14. In reality, only two thirds of India's children go to school.

Why don't all children go? For most, the answer is simple. There is no school in their village. For other families, the children are too important as workers to be allowed the luxury of school. Even those who begin first grade often do not go beyond the fourth grade. Fewer girls than boys go to school. Some families in villages feel that educating girls is a waste of time.

For those who continue their education, learning English is necessary. Most teaching in high schools is in English. Because many Indians do not speak English, they are unable to attend high school. In addition, students in high school take tests at the end of every year. If they do well, they go on. If not, their schooling is over. The amount of schooling they complete decides their future.

Recently, India has opened more technical schools. Technical skills will help India's people find answers to the problems their country faces.

On Assignment...
Imagine that you have visited Bombay. What would you say about it in your letters home?

Section 2 Review

1. What is a bustee?
2. **Drawing Conclusions** How is education in India different from education in the United States?

SECTION 3

The Arts and Literature in South Asia

How does religion influence the arts and literature in South Asia?

The Indian subcontinent has a rich tradition of art, literature, music, and drama. Most of it is linked to religion. Two thousand years ago, artists who worked in gold crafted figures of gods. Buddhists built **stupas** in the 200s B.C. These dome-shaped burial mounds contain the remains of holy people, including Buddha. Buddhists visit these sacred sites.

Later, Hindus built and decorated temples. Gods with many arms, marching elephants, and prancing horses cover the walls of these temples. Hindus are also known for their

Chapter 3

skillfully executed miniature paintings. These tiny, colorful paintings show scenes from Hindu stories.

Muslims brought a new style of art to the subcontinent. Islamic arches and domes appeared in mosques and other buildings. The Taj Mahal, with its arches and graceful spaces, is one example.

Dance and Music

The performing arts in India are also linked to religion. Indian dance comes from traditions that are at least 4,000 years old. It takes a minimum of ten years to train for some kinds of traditional dance. There are about 140 different poses a dancer must learn. Just as important is learning complete control over the muscles in the face, neck, and hands. Each arched eyebrow has a meaning. Indian dancers wear beautiful and rich costumes. Many of the dances are based on Hindu stories.

Indian music is based on a very complicated system of notes and melodies. Each piece of music is based on a **raga** (RAH-gah). A raga is a traditional melody that recalls an emotion or a season. There are 70,000 ragas. Indian music is often played on stringed and wind instruments. Indians also use drums in their music.

Literature

The earliest Indian literature was poetry. It was passed orally from generation to generation. Then it was written in Sanskrit. These early poems were religious. The *Mahabharata,* which is still important to Hindus, is one example of an **epic** poem. An epic is a very long poem that tells the story of a hero. Another important epic is the *Ramayana.* One lesson in this epic is that people should honor their parents.

Later works were based on themes such as love and war. Some poems were written in other languages. A romance called *The Jeweled Anklet* is a long poem that was written in the Tamil language. Both Tamil and Sanskrit are ancient Indian languages that were used to write poems, plays, and stories.

In modern times, one outstanding Indian writer was Sir Rabindranath Tagore. He lived from 1861 to 1941. Tagore wrote hundreds of popular Indian songs, in addition to poems, short stories, novels, and plays. In 1913, he was the first Asian to win the Nobel Prize for Literature.

Section 3 Review

1. How did Indian literature change over the centuries?
2. **Determining Cause and Effect** What was the effect of religion on the arts in India?

Traditional Indian dance requires dancers to learn about 140 poses. To perform dances based on Hindu stories, dancers must know hand gestures called mudras.

Case Study 3

The Hollywood of India

There is a term for most of the movies made in Bombay—*masala*. It means "spicy mixture." These movies first became popular in the 1970s. There is a beautiful woman, a handsome man who wants to win her, and a bad guy who wants to make trouble. There is comedy, action and adventure, and dancing and singing.

"Indians like to cry at the movies," Rishi Kapoor told *National Geographic Magazine*. "So our movies are like soap operas." Despite the tears, though, there is always a happy ending.

Romance is a critical part of these movies. In a land where most marriages are arranged, romance is always appealing. There's no kissing, though. Most Indians think that it is not proper to show kissing in public.

Satyajit Ray

There are some Indian and Pakistani filmmakers whose work is well known outside their countries. Perhaps the most famous is a filmmaker named Satyajit Ray. Ray began his career as an artist for an advertising agency. In the 1950s, he made *Pather Panchali* (*Song of the Road*). The movie, which Ray made without professional actors, was the first of a series of three movies that were to make him known throughout the world.

These three movies told the story of Apu, a boy whose family moves from the country to the city. The work is known as the *Apu Trilogy*. The movies were a real look at the way people live. Just before Ray died in 1992, he won an American Academy Award for his life's work.

Case Study Review

1. What does *masala* mean and why is it a good term to describe Indian movies?
2. **Comparing and Contrasting** How do you think the movies of Satyajit Ray are different from most of the movies that are made for Indian audiences?

On Assignment...

How would you describe an Indian movie to friends at home?

REVIEWING CHAPTER 3

I. Reviewing Vocabulary

Match each word on the left with the correct definition on the right.

1. bustee
2. stupa
3. raga
4. epic

a. a poor area of a city where people live in shacks
b. one of the ancient melody patterns of Indian music
c. a long poem that tells the story of a hero
d. a dome-shaped burial mound that serves as a Buddhist holy shrine

II. Understanding the Chapter

Answer the questions below on a separate sheet of paper.

1. How have women's roles changed in India?
2. What have been the results of population growth in India? How has the government tried to control population growth?
3. Why are there many Indians who do not know how to read and write?
4. Explain the difficulties involved in becoming an Indian dancer.

III. Building Skills: Comparing and Contrasting

Write a sentence comparing and contrasting the items in each pair below.

1. (a) life in villages (b) life in the cities
2. (a) the population of the United States (b) the population of India
3. (a) education for poor children in India (b) education for wealthy children in India

IV. Working Together

Work with a group to write and perform a skit about life in India. Use the story about Keval and Geeta in Section 1 as a model. Then choose a topic from the chapter and decide on the scene and characters you will portray. Possibilities include: life in a rural village, life in a bustee, training as an Indian dancer, or the movie industry in Bombay. Use library resources to find out more about your topic.

On Assignment...

Writing Letters: Review the notes you took as you read this chapter. You will write one letter to your family and one to a friend. What will you tell each about India in your letters?

Tea leaves are picked and then dried for brewing the flavorful beverage. India is one of the world's leading producers of tea, exporting it around the world.

CHAPTER 4

South Asia in the World Today

What challenges has South Asia faced since World War II?

Looking at Key Terms

- **martial law** temporary rule by the military
- **militant** a person who believes in using violence to promote a cause
- **communism** an economic system in which the government owns and controls most property and industry
- **non-alignment** a policy of not being allied with other nations on a regular basis, but of deciding each question of foreign policy individually
- **neutrality** a policy of refusing to take sides in a conflict
- **pact** an agreement
- **coup** a revolt, often by military leaders, against a nation's government

On Assignment...

Creating an Illustrated Time Line: In this chapter, you will organize the information you learn by making an illustrated time line that shows key events in South Asia from the 1940s to the present. Time lines list events in the order in which they occurred. Three or four events on your time line will be accompanied by pictures. Look for hint boxes to help you choose items for your time line.

SECTION 1

India's Government and Economy

What challenges have India's government and economy faced since independence?

India is the world's largest democracy. Its government is patterned after Britain's government. In both countries, a prime minister is the most powerful government official. There are a president and a vice president, but their jobs are mostly ceremonial. They do not hold much real power.

In the United States, Congress makes the laws. Like the United States, India has a lawmaking body that is divided into two houses. The Indian lawmaking body is a parliament.

All Indian citizens who are 18 and over are permitted to vote. There are no restrictions based on caste or education. Because almost half of India's voters cannot read or write, symbols are used to represent the different parties. For example, the Praja Socialist party's symbol is a thatched hut. The symbol of the National Congress party is a team of oxen.

In India, as in Great Britain and other countries, people in each district vote for representatives to parliament. The party that wins the most seats chooses the prime minister.

The National Congress Party

For its first 20 years, India was controlled by the same political party, the National Congress party. For much of this time, the party was led by Jawaharlal Nehru (jah•WAH•hahr•lahl NAY•roo). Nehru was a leader during India's fight for independence. He became president of the Independent Congress party (INC) in 1929. INC became the National Congress party after independence.

Nehru led the Congress party and remained prime minister of India until his death in 1964. During his time in office, Nehru led his new country well. He introduced an economic plan that helped farmers produce more food. He also helped India to build new industries.

After Nehru died, Lal Bahadur Shastri became leader of the Congress party. He soon faced a huge problem. In 1965, India and Pakistan went to war. Both claimed Kashmir, in the northwest. Within a few weeks, the war ended. The following year, Shastri signed a peace treaty with Pakistan's leader. A few hours later, Shastri died of a heart attack.

India's next leader was Nehru's daughter, Indira Gandhi. The fact that a woman was chosen as leader surprised many. It seemed to say that India was moving into a new era. At first, Gandhi faced tough times. India's economy was in a shambles. People were hungry and were loudly protesting against the government. The country was suffering from drought, a period during which there is little or no rain. By 1969, though, India was producing more food. In addition, the birth rate was lower, so there were fewer mouths to feed.

Gandhi's greatest problem was the continuous fighting between India's religious and ethnic groups. At one point, she declared **martial law**. When a country is under martial law, its military enforces all laws and maintains order. In addition, Gandhi put some of her opponents in jail and restricted a number of freedoms. It seemed as if India's democracy was being replaced by a dictatorship.

In 1977, Gandhi held an election, which she lost. For the first time, India was ruled by a party other than the Congress party. The Janata party won the election and its leader, Morarji Desai, became prime minister. That didn't last, though. In three years, Gandhi was back in power.

Gandhi and the Sikhs

In the early 1980s, the Sikhs in Punjab began to demand their own country. They wanted to create an independent state in Punjab. In 1984, the conflict exploded into

Rajiv Gandhi waves to a crowd. Behind him are pictures of India's great leaders. From left to right are Indira Gandhi, Mohandas Gandhi, and Jawaharlal Nehru.

violence. Sikhs took over the Golden Temple at Amritsar, their holiest place. Gandhi sent soldiers to drive the Sikhs out of the temple. More than 600 Sikhs were killed in the fighting. India's population of 14 million Sikhs was outraged. Sikhs serving in the Indian army rebelled. On October 31, 1984, several Sikh bodyguards shot and killed the prime minister.

More Trouble Indira Gandhi's son Rajiv became the next head of the Congress party. In 1987, he sent Indian troops to neighboring Sri Lanka to keep the peace. Different groups in that country were fighting for control. (See Section 2.) Gandhi left office in 1989, but he decided in 1991 to try to return to power. While campaigning for that election, he was assassinated by a bomb planted by a Sri Lankan group.

In 1991, P.V. Narasimha Rao took office. He became prime minister during a troubled time in India. The economy was in decline and the Soviet Union, one of India's allies, was collapsing. In addition, Rao seemed an unlikely choice for prime minister. He did not seem ambitious and his health was not good.

Rao, however, surprised people. He worked with intelligence and firmness to address India's problems. In economics and foreign policy, he boldly ended outdated policies, replacing them with new ones.

In 1993, Rao faced new challenges when Hindu **militants** destroyed a 16th-century Islamic mosque. A militant is a person who believes in using violence as a way to promote a cause. The militants said that the mosque had been the site of a Hindu temple. Riots broke out. Almost 2,000 people were killed.

Today, the different faiths and peoples of India maintain an uneasy peace. Yet there is much hope for the future.

Economic Challenges

India faces serious economic challenges. It has a high potential for industrial and electric power development. There are large deposits of valuable minerals, such as iron ore and coal. However, India has not been able to reach its potential. It is one of the world's poorest countries. More than one half of its people cannot read or write. Why is India in this situation?

Chapter 4

Agriculture employs about 70 percent of India's people. Indian farmers need water for their crops to grow. These workers are building a canal in Durgapur, India, that will direct water to the fields.

Agriculture Farming is the occupation of 70 percent of India's people. Most still farm their land the way their parents, and their grandparents, did. There is much to be said for these traditional ways of farming, though. If climate conditions are right, India can usually raise enough food for its ever-growing population.

India's farmers, however, face serious problems. One problem is the destruction that is caused by plant diseases and rats. Also, many farmers do not have enough fertilizer or water for their crops. All this means that the amount of food per acre that farmers can grow is smaller than in other countries.

Debt is another problem for Indian farmers. They borrow during bad years and have trouble repaying the loans.

The government has tried to deal with these problems. It has built dams and has tried to get more modern equipment for farmers. Many of the government's plans have been successful. Farmers grow much more food now. In fact, India exports more food than it imports. Economists think, though, that resolving these problems can increase the amount of food that Indian farmers harvest.

Industry When the British ran India, there were many factories. They produced rubber, glass, paper, cotton, and steel. During World War II, those plants became very important. They made war goods, such as airplanes and ships.

When India won its independence from Britain, its main goal was building industry. India built new cotton mills and steel plants. Today India boasts that it makes steel more cheaply than any country in the world. Mining coal has been important. Coal is burned for electricity. Homes are heated and factories are run by coal energy.

India has a long history of "cottage industries," or businesses whose goods are produced by people working at home. Spinning and weaving cotton are cottage industries. About 6.3 million people work in

On Assignment...

Note the important events in this section on your time line. Also note any ideas for illustrations.

manufacturing industries. However, more than 20 million work in cottage industries.

India's industries have greatly increased production since World War II. Basically, though, India is still a farming country. Only one fifth of the money in India comes from mining and manufacturing goods. Much of the rest comes from agriculture.

Section 1 Review

1. What are the problems farmers face in India?
2. **Analyzing Information** Imagine that you are India's leader right after World War II. Which problem would you tackle first? Why?

SECTION 2

Other Nations of South Asia

Why did Pakistan and Bangladesh separate?

"You want to know about Pakistan?" Aziz is sitting at a small cafe in Karachi. He is stirring his tea with a tiny spoon. "It is a story of bloodshed. It is a story of drama. Bangladesh, too. Talk to my friend Ali. He is from Bangladesh. He will tell you." Ali, a thin, serious-looking man, nods.

Pakistan and Bangladesh

"Pakistan and Bangladesh were once one country," Aziz says. "And once, we were all part of India. After World War II, India won

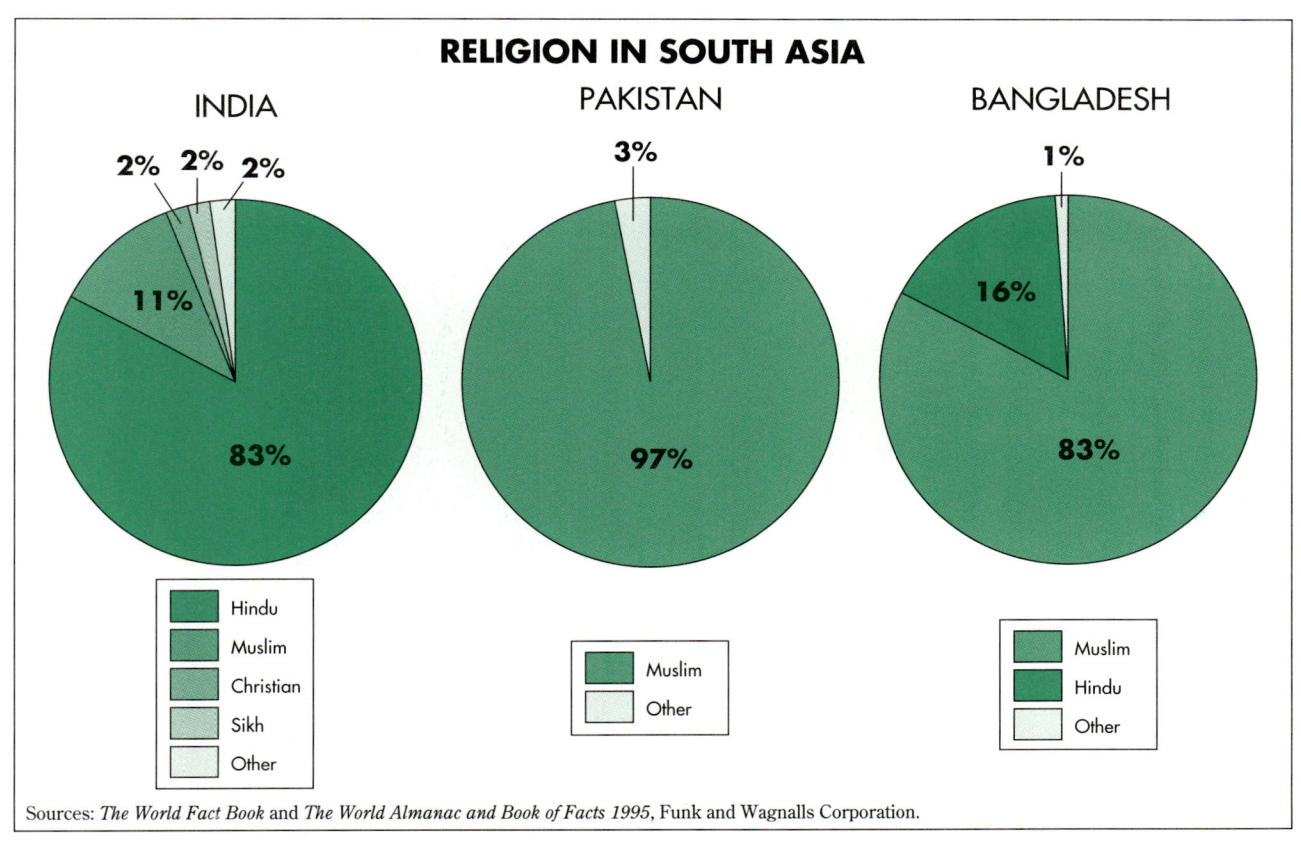

RELIGION IN SOUTH ASIA

INDIA: Hindu 83%, Muslim 11%, Christian 2%, Sikh 2%, Other 2%

PAKISTAN: Muslim 97%, Other 3%

BANGLADESH: Muslim 83%, Hindu 16%, Other 1%

Sources: *The World Fact Book* and *The World Almanac and Book of Facts 1995*, Funk and Wagnalls Corporation.

Hinduism and Islam have the largest number of followers in South Asia today. Which country has the largest percentage of Hindus? Which country has the largest percentage of Muslims?

Chapter 4

its independence. A man named Muhammad Ali Jinnah would not let Pakistan become part of India. Ali Jinnah was from what is now Pakistan. He was part of the Congress party of India.

"He and I—most Pakistanis—are Muslim, you see. Most people in India are Hindu. In the 1930s, Ali Jinnah began to argue that the Hindus paid no attention to the problems of the Muslims. He quit the Congress party and became president of the Muslim League. He understood that we needed our own state. Ali Jinnah was stubborn. He would not let India take us. So Pakistan became its own country in 1947."

Aziz keeps stirring his tea, and sighs. "Things might have been different if Ali Jinnah had not died in 1948. Then, Liaquat Ali Khan became Pakistan's president. He had headaches. Many headaches." Aziz counts the headaches on his fingers. "There was Kashmir. Both India and Pakistan claimed it. Then there was the fact that East Pakistan and West Pakistan were separated by about 1,000 miles.

"The worst thing, though, was the panic. Muslims scrambled to leave India. Hindus scrambled to leave Pakistan. More than 15 million people moved. Of these, perhaps a half million died. Hindus and Muslims killed each other. It was a terrible time.

"After that, there were more problems. Did you know that there was a revolution in 1958? Well, the army took over and army Field Marshal Ayub Khan became president. There was some peace then. In 1962, we got a new constitution. Ayub Khan may have taken over by force, but he was a good leader. He set up a better government. It was based in the villages. He set up a plan for the economy to grow."

Aziz stopped to take a breath. Then he continued, "In 1965, Ayub Khan was elected to the presidency again. He faced more problems. The biggest, the worst, was the trouble between East Pakistan and West Pakistan."

"Those were bad times," Ali breaks in, shaking his head. "Much hatred. My people—the people in the east—felt we should have more say. There are more of us and we are poorer than the West Pakistanis. Then, too, the army was mostly in the west. We felt unprotected. There were riots in East Pakistan in the late 1960s. Ayub Khan was forced out in 1971. Then, there was martial law.

Bangladeshi soldiers ride atop a tank near Jessore, Pakistan, in 1971. Tensions ran high as East Pakistan declared independence from West Pakistan. In 1971, East Pakistan became Bangladesh and West Pakistan became Pakistan.

"Soldiers from West Pakistan were sent to East Pakistan to put down the riots. The army could not control things, so it began killing. Soldiers killed tens of thousands of East Pakistanis!" Ali says angrily. "Of course we revolted! There was war. India joined with us. They did it, probably, because millions of East Pakistanis fled to India. The Pakistanis did it to keep from getting killed. Anyway, we, the people of the east, won. And we no longer called ourselves Pakistani. In 1971, we became the new nation of Bangladesh. Pakistan now is what was once called West Pakistan."

Aziz is looking at Ali with a slight smile. "You can still get angry about all this, old friend. But now we are two nations. Surely we can be friends?"

Ali smiles a small smile. "You must forgive me. It is not so long ago, after all. I, like many, lost family and friends during that time. But you are right. And time does move on."

"Let us see," Aziz says. "Today Pakistan has a democracy. Since 1988, we have had free elections. And you, Ali? What do you see for Bangladesh?"

"We have had a hard time, as you know," Ali says. "We began life as a country with very little money. Things were in a shambles. Then, in 1974, we had the worst floods in two decades. There wasn't enough food. One leader, Major General Zia, was killed in 1981. In 1991, his widow, Begun Khalid Zia, became prime minister. A cyclone killed thousands in 1993. Then we had to take in Muslim refugees fleeing Burma. In Bangladesh, sometimes it seems we pick ourselves up just in time to be knocked down again. But we will get through this, too. We will make our nation."

Sri Lanka

Fringed palm trees rise from sandy shores. Sri Lanka is an island nation located southeast of India. It is a beautiful place. It looks like a tourist's paradise. But bitter fights between groups have scared away visitors.

Many people come to climb the Himalaya mountains. Some come for adventure. Here, a group of Hindus makes a religious pilgrimage to the Amarnath Cave.

The first people to come to Sri Lanka were the Sinhalese from northern India. They came in the 500s B.C. On Sri Lanka, they met the Veddas and conquered them. The island was then called Sinhala. Two hundred years later, the Sinhalese converted to Buddhism.

In the A.D. 200s, Tamil kings from southern India came to the island. They made a Hindu kingdom in the north. The Portuguese, the Dutch, and the British came much later—in the 1500s. In 1796, the island became a British colony called Ceylon. It became famous for the tea that grew there on plantations.

After World War II, the people of Ceylon wanted independence from Britain. It happened at the same time India became a state,

Chapter 4

in 1947. Then, in 1972, the country changed its name to Sri Lanka. Since its founding, violence between the Hindu Tamils and the Sinhalese has marked its history. The Sinhalese had more power than the Tamils. The Tamils resented this, and fought for their own country on the island.

In the 1980s, terrorism and fighting became common. In February 1989, more than 1,000 people died in the violence. The 1990s have not brought peace. In May 1993, President Ranasinghe Premadasa was killed by a bomb. The following year, in a landslide victory, Chandrika Kumaratunga became Sri Lanka's first woman prime minister. In her campaign, she promised to end the "culture of assassination" that plagued her country.

Bhutan and Nepal

Set in the mountains, the countries of Bhutan and Nepal lie north of India, between India and China. Both countries are ruled by kings.

Nepal is larger than Bhutan. It is about 54,000 square miles (139,860 sq km) in size and has a population of more than 20 million people. Until recent times, the mountains isolated Nepal from the world. Its people lived a traditional lifestyle. The king even banned political parties. In 1990, though, he ended this ban. The first democratic election in 32 years was held in May 1991.

Nepal is a popular spot for tourists. They come to climb the highest mountain on earth, Mount Everest, and to enjoy the beauty of the country. They also come to see the ancient ways of the people.

The money that tourists bring is welcome. Nepal is a very poor country. Only 10 percent of its people can read and write. Some Nepalese make a living by joining the Indian army.

Bhutan is ruled by a king who has complete control of his country's affairs. However, Bhutan signed a treaty with India agreeing to consult India about foreign affairs. Bhutan is about 18,000 square miles (46,646 sq km) and contains about 1.4 million people. The people of Bhutan are related to the people of Tibet.

On Assignment...

Scan this section, noting the important dates. Next to each date, write why it is important.

The leader of Bhutan is called the Dragon King. He is the grandson of the first Dragon King, who took power in 1907. The Dragon King holds power, but he has a group of advisers. India directs Bhutan's defense and foreign policy.

Bhutan's Dragon King has tried to keep the country isolated. In 1988, most tourists were banned. In 1990, a law was passed that forbids people from watching TV programs from other countries. Like the people of Nepal, most people in Bhutan cannot read or write.

Section 2 Review

1. Why did East Pakistan and West Pakistan separate into two countries?
2. **Comparing and Contrasting** What do Bhutan and Nepal have in common? How are they different?

SECTION 3

South Asia and the World

What role do India and Pakistan play in world politics?

After World War II, there emerged two major powers in the world: the United States and the Soviet Union (USSR). The two countries competed to win allies. Some countries adopted **communism** and allied themselves with the Soviet Union. Other countries rejected communism and allied themselves with the United States. Still others decided to follow a different course. India was one of these nations.

Nehru, India's prime minister after the war, decided on a policy of **non-alignment**. In each individual foreign policy situation, India would decide how to act. Many countries that won their independence after the war agreed with India. They too adopted a policy of non-alignment. This policy, Nehru said, was different from **neutrality**. Neutral countries do not take sides in a conflict.

The policy of non-alignment made some people in the United States angry. The United States gave aid to India, people reasoned. How could India refuse to become its permanent ally? India, however, stuck to its position. Non-alignment meant that India voted to let China join the United Nations. The United States voted against it. India also refused to vote with the United States against the Soviet Union when it invaded Hungary.

India hoped that a policy of non-alignment would allow it to be on friendly terms with all nations. Based on this idea, the Soviet Union and India built strong ties. There were several reasons for this.

- The two countries were located close to each other in Asia.
- India admired the Soviet Union's attempts to get its economy moving.
- The leaders of the two countries were friendly.
- The two countries had some problems in common. Both were trying to build industry and farming.
- The Soviet Union gave India more than $1 billion in aid. This money was used to buy food and to build industry.

In 1954, the friendship between India and the United States cooled. In that year, Pakistan joined the United States in a **pact**, or agreement, against the Soviet Union. India saw that pact as a threat to its security.

The United States was also upset when India began to build nuclear weapons. The United States saw that as a danger. India said that having a nuclear bomb would help it keep the world peaceful.

In 1971, the United States supported Pakistan in the civil war that led to the creation of Bangladesh. This angered India. Since then, the United States and India have had an uneasy relationship.

Economic Challenges

In 1991, though, India announced a new policy. It decided to move away from a socialist economy, in which the government owned and controlled most big industries, to a capitalist economy, in which private individuals own and run most industries. India did this in hopes of attracting foreign investors. Foreign investors, India hoped, would pump money into its economy by building new businesses and creating new jobs.

Trouble With China

China and India became neighbors when China took over Tibet in 1950. Until 1959, the two countries were good neighbors. India supported China's admission to the United Nations. China was grateful for that.

In 1959, though, the people of Tibet rebelled against China. The Dalai Lama, the leader of Tibet, fled to India. Then Chinese troops took over some Indian land. India asked China to leave. China replied that India had encouraged Tibet to revolt.

The relationship between India and China remained uneasy. In 1962, China invaded India. Both Britain and the United States sent help to India. China stopped attacking, but it kept much of the land that it had taken. Today, China still holds that land.

Pakistan and the World

Pakistan has generally allied itself with the United States. In 1950, Liaquat Ali Khan, Pakistan's president, visited President Harry Truman. This angered the Soviet

In the late 1970s, millions of refugees from Afghanistan fled to Pakistan to escape the horrors of war in their country. Pakistanis did their best to help the refugees during their stay.

Union. Then Pakistan accepted aid from the United States.

As you read earlier, in 1954, Pakistan signed a pact with the United States against the Soviet Union. The move made relations between Pakistan and India even more strained. It also soured the friendship between the United States and India.

In 1979, Pakistan began to build nuclear weapons. The United States became angry with its ally. Pakistan's leader, General Zia, refused to stop, however. President Jimmy Carter cut off U.S. aid to Pakistan. Then, in 1979, the Soviet Union invaded Afghanistan. The Soviets hoped that Afghanistan would remain a Communist state. Afghanistan and Pakistan share a border.

On Assignment...

Find at least three important dates in this section and write them on your list. Be sure to explain why these dates are important.

The United States joined the fight against the Soviets. It used Pakistan to give money to the Afghanis. More than 2.5 million Afghan refugees streamed into Pakistan. The Afghanis were poor, sick, disabled, and homeless. Many were taken in by individual Pakistanis. The Pakistani government also helped. In addition, the United States sent $3.2 billion to aid the refugees. With the collapse of the Soviet Union, however, there is no longer a need for the United States to send money to stop the spread of communism.

The war in Afghanistan upset the flow of life in Pakistan. Then the Persian Gulf War in 1990–1991 caused more problems. Thousands of Pakistanis who worked in the Middle East had to return home. That created a huge problem because the money these workers sent back to Pakistan had helped the country. Now, no money from the Middle East was coming to Pakistan.

Pakistan continues to face challenges. Natural disasters are a fact of life. So is overpopulation. Pakistan's need for outside aid is still strong. Its future role in the world is still to be determined.

Section 3 Review

1. Why were both the United States and the Soviet Union unsatisfied with India's policy of non-alignment?
2. **Summarizing** Explain why India and the Soviet Union had close ties.

Case Study 4

Benazir Bhutto:
The First Islamic Woman Leader

It was 1977. Benazir Bhutto, the beautiful daughter of Pakistan's leader, Ali Bhutto, was coming home. The time that she had spent in the West had been a triumph. Now, she was ready to join her country's foreign service.

Days after she arrived, her father was forced out in a military **coup**, or revolt, against the nation's government. Pakistan's new leader, General Zia, held her father in a tiny, dark, cold, jail cell. In 1979, he ordered Ali Bhutto hanged. Fearing that Ali's daughter Benazir would rally the people, Zia held her under house arrest for four years. Finally, in 1984, Zia allowed her to travel to England for treatment of an ear infection.

In 1986, Benazir Bhutto returned. In shock, she watched as three million people met her at the airport. "Jeevat Bhutto!" they shouted, throwing rose petals. "Long live Bhutto!"

For two years, Bhutto worked to rebuild her father's party. She married, and she was pregnant with her first child when Zia called an election for the post of prime minister. He may have reasoned that Bhutto, who was eight months pregnant, would not campaign.

He was wrong. Then, three months before the election, Zia died in a plane crash. In November, Bhutto's party won the most seats. Bhutto found herself the first Islamic woman leader in modern times.

Bhutto restored democracy. She released political prisoners and allowed a free press. She built close ties to other countries and started a bank that helped Pakistani business. But Bhutto's party had a slim margin in the National Assembly. It could not pass laws.

Then, in 1990, the president of Pakistan dismissed her. He was head of another political party. He charged her with corruption. Friends of Bhutto's husband may have made money from the government. However, the charges were not proven.

Bhutto became a leader of the opposition party. In 1993, she was again elected prime minister. In the Islamic world, where women are often not heard or seen, she blazed a trail.

Case Study Review

1. What changes did Benazir Bhutto make when she was elected prime minister of Pakistan?
2. **Drawing Conclusions** Why do you think Bhutto was able to become the first Islamic woman leader?

REVIEWING CHAPTER 4

I. Reviewing Vocabulary
Match each word on the left with the correct definition on the right.

1. coup
2. non-alignment
3. neutrality
4. militant

a. a person who believes in using violence to win a cause
b. a policy of refusing to take sides in a conflict
c. a revolt, often by military leaders, against a nation's government
d. a policy of not being allied with other nations on a regular basis

II. Understanding the Chapter
Answer the questions below on a separate sheet of paper.

1. How do most Indians make a living?
2. Why did East Pakistan become Bangladesh?
3. What is the difference between non-alignment and neutrality?
4. Why was Benazir Bhutto forced from office in 1990?

III. Building Skills: Identifying Places
Name the country that is best described by each sentence.

1. This is the most crowded country in the world.
2. The Tamils and the Sinhalese still fight over this country.
3. This country is the home of the highest mountain in the world.
4. This is the largest democracy in the world.
5. This country was formed in 1971 from part of Pakistan.

IV. Working Together
In groups of four, choose a country in South Asia and write questions about that country on cards. Write the answers on the back of the cards. Each group should take turns asking its questions of the whole class.

On Assignment...
Creating an Illustrated Time Line: You should now have a list of at least ten key events. Arrange these events in chronological, or time, order. Now, choose two or three to illustrate. Create original drawings, or use photocopies or pictures from old newspapers and magazines. Present your time line to the class, explaining your reasons for choosing each event.

CHAPTER 5

The Heritage of Southeast Asia

What groups of people had the largest impact on Southeast Asia?

Hinduism is part of Southeast Asia's heritage. Traders from India brought the religion to the region. Today, Hinduism has large numbers of followers in several countries in Southeast Asia.

Looking at Key Terms

- **migrate** to move from one place to another
- **revolt** an uprising
- **canal** a ditch made by humans to carry water
- **animism** the belief that spirits live in the natural world in such things as rocks, trees, and streams
- **colony** a land that is controlled by another country
- **guerrilla warfare** hit-and-run attacks by small bands of fighters against a larger power

On Assignment...

Creating a Mini-History: Your assignment is to create a "mini-history" of Southeast Asia for students in the third grade. As you read this chapter, take notes, especially about events and people you think would interest third graders. Consider, too, how you would use illustrations to help students understand the history of Southeast Asia. Look for hint boxes to help you take notes. At the end of the chapter you will put your mini-history together.

SECTION 1

Early Civilizations of Southeast Asia

What were the characteristics of early Southeast Asian civilizations?

The young prince stood up proudly. The shirt he wore was so dazzling that the maker hid when she wove it so she could keep her methods secret. "The clothes were so fine they rippled when the wind blew," the Philippine story reads. "They were woven from thread spun from the finest gold. This golden thread was mixed with the smoothest of silk threads." And the prince? "He looked so well in them, shining as bright as a star in the sky."

The Maranaos in the Philippines were one of many groups in ancient Southeast Asia. For their rulers, jewels, gold, and spices were part of life. This part of the world has many riches.

As you have read, these riches are one reason that so many outsiders came to Southeast Asia. Another reason is its location. Mainland Southeast Asia is close to China and India. Indian merchants came at first to trade. Some decided to stay and make the region their home. People from China **migrated**, or moved there, from the mainland. Some continued to migrate, spreading into the islands. Still others sailed to the islands from other regions.

Many small kingdoms in Southeast Asia rose and fell. Several great kingdoms held power for centuries.

The Kingdoms of Vietnam

China and Vietnam have shared a long history. The Chinese ruled the area from 100 B.C. to A.D. 900. The Vietnamese sometimes revolted against the Chinese. The most famous **revolt**, or uprising, was led by the two Trung sisters in A.D. 39. For two years, they ruled. When the Chinese regained control, the sisters jumped to their deaths in the Day River.

During the 1,000 years of Chinese rule, the Vietnamese adopted some Chinese ways. The Vietnamese were influenced by Chinese religion, language, art, and poetry. In 939, the Vietnamese people broke away from China and formed the kingdom of Dai Viet. It lasted for nearly 1,000 years.

The Pagan Kingdom

People came to Myanmar (Burma) from India, Tibet, and China, building the Pagan (pah•GAHN) kingdom in the 800s. King Anawrahta and his son made the Pagan kingdom rich. The villagers paid taxes to the king.

Buddhism spread and became the kingdom's chief religion. The Pagan kingdom lasted until 1287. In that year, Mongol armies from China marched in and took over. It was not until the 1400s that the Burmese regained control of their country.

The Angkor Kingdom

A legend tells of an Indian prince who had a vision that he was to explore the South China Sea. When he reached Cambodia, a princess rowed out in a canoe to meet him. The prince shot an arrow through the boat. The legend says that the princess was thrilled with his daring. She promptly married him.

Although this story is only a legend, India did indeed influence Cambodia. Cambodia's system of writing is based on an Indian language. In its early history, Cambodians also adopted Hinduism, the religion that you read about in Chapter 2.

The glorious history of the Angkor kingdom began in 802. In that year, King Jayavarman stood on a mountain and declared himself a god king. He said that he would bring the rains and that he would bring happiness. For 250 years, the Angkor kings performed

Angkor Wat was originally built as a Hindu temple. Constructed from 1112 to 1152, it is the largest religious building in the world. Its highest point rises 200 feet (61 m) and it is surrounded by a moat that measures almost 2.5 miles (4 km) in circumference.

ceremonies to bring rain, riches, and happiness to their kingdom.

The kings wore silk clothing and gold jewelry. They were thought to be gods. Thousands of servants made their every wish come true. All the kings had to do was convince the spirits to bring good weather and to keep the earth spinning.

The Angkor kings built a series of Hindu temples. They are among the treasures of the world. One, Angkor Wat, is the largest religious building in the world. In 1860, hundreds of years after the decline of the Angkor kingdom, a Frenchman stumbled upon the temple of Angkor Wat. He was stunned by the temple's beauty. "It is grander than anything left us by Greece and Rome," he wrote.

The Angkor kings built and controlled Cambodia's water system. They constructed **canals** for farming. A canal is a ditch that is made to carry water. Cambodia's water system kept the area from flooding and stored water for the dry season. As a result, Cambodians grew much rice.

The golden time, however, did not last long. In the 1100s, the rulers began to ask too much of their people. Then the water system broke down. Malaria and plague struck. In 1431, Thailand fought for Angkor and won. The Cambodians left Angkor. Jungle grew over the wonders of Angkor and Angkor Wat. (See Case Study 6 on page 69 for more information about Angkor Wat.)

The Thai Kingdoms

There had always been small kingdoms in Thailand. The first unified Thai kingdom arose in 1350. One reason it did well was that the Mongols moved into Southeast Asia. Many of the other kingdoms in the area were destroyed. That gave the kingdom of Ayutthaya the chance to flourish and expand its territory. It existed for 400 years. During that time, as you learned, it conquered Cambodia.

The founder of Ayutthaya, Rama Tibodi, set laws for his people. The laws allowed slavery and they allowed men to have more than one wife. Officials in the government were severely punished if they stole money from the people.

This kingdom lasted until the Burmese attacked in 1767. Four years later, the Thais revolted. Their leader, General Pya Taksin, declared himself king. On his death, Pya Chakkri (CHAHK•kree) took the throne. To this day, the kings of Thailand are his descendants.

The Kingdoms of Indonesia

Indonesia's ancient kingdoms were based on trade. The first grand empire was the Sri Vijaya (shree vah•JIH•yah). From the 600s to the 1200s, it controlled trade in the region.

Sri Vijaya was located in Sumatra. When it was most powerful, in about A.D. 1000, it also held most of Java and Borneo. The clue to the kingdom's success was the Strait of Malacca. The strait was the shortest way between the Indian and Pacific oceans. (See the map on pages 94–95.)

Through the strait, trading ships carried the treasures of the world. Gold, jewels, and spices were all carried on the ships. The wealth also attracted pirates, who were a constant threat. They hid in coves in the shadows of palm trees and attacked.

The kings of Sri Vijaya used many methods to stay in control of Indonesia. They maintained a huge fleet of ships to keep order. Sri Vijaya's kings also demanded high fees from the ships that sailed through their waters.

In the 1200s, the mighty Sri Vijaya kingdom faded. Other kingdoms took over trade. The most famous may be the Majapahit, which was based in Java. It lasted from about 1300 to the early 1500s. At its height, it controlled almost all of Indonesia and most of Malaysia.

The Role of Religion

The religions of outsiders had an impact on Southeast Asia. Probably the first was Hinduism, brought by traders from India. Buddhism, also from India, spread to Mainland Southeast Asia. (See the map on page 24.) Today it is the main religion of Myanmar, Cambodia, Thailand, Vietnam, and Laos.

Islam had a strong impact in the area. Arab traders brought this religion to Southeast Asia in about A.D. 900. Today Islam is the main religion in Indonesia, Brunei, and Malaysia. Indonesia is in fact the largest Islamic country in the world. It is an Islamic country unlike any other, though, because many Indonesian Muslims mix Islam with traditional island religions. The most popular traditional religion is **animism**. Animists believe that spirits live in trees, rocks, and streams. In Indonesia, it is not unusual to see a Muslim who both worships his ancestors and prays to the spirits in water.

On Assignment...

What facts about the ancient kingdoms of Southeast Asia would you include in your mini-history for third graders? Make sketches of drawings that you could include in your book.

Missionaries also came to Southeast Asia to convert people to Christianity. They had little impact, though. The only country in the region that is mostly Christian is the Philippines.

Section 1 Review

1. How did India and China influence the early kingdoms of Southeast Asia?
2. **Making Inferences** Why do you think the Angkor kingdom collapsed?

SECTION 2

Europeans Colonize the Region

How did Europeans gain control of most of Southeast Asia in the 1800s?

Spices! The seaman closed his eyes and breathed in the rich smells of clove, nutmeg, and cinnamon. This will make us all rich, he thought. The sailors had found a source for the spices that Europe needed. And they had an ocean route. No more paying Arab traders high prices for spices. This was a day to celebrate. Europe was hungry for spices. With them, food could be kept much longer. In the time before refrigerators, preserving food was very important.

The search for spices led to contacts between Europe and Southeast Asia. The

Case Study 5

The Myths of Indonesia

It is an epic battle between good and evil. The two men playing the part of the Barong come out first. The mythical creature has a huge head. Its wide eyes and bared teeth gleam. Down its back spills tangled fur and hair. A gold headdress shines from its head. Rangda, the witch, faces the Barong. Rangda is evil. Her tongue is a flame. Her face is set in a terrible sneer. She wears a necklace of human body parts. The two face off in a dance of death. Men armed with daggers come under Rangda's spell. They fall into a trance. Then they stab themselves with their daggers. The Barong protects the men. As much as they stab, they cannot hurt themselves. In the end, the Barong always wins.

This Balinese myth is acted out in a dance. Like many Indonesian myths, this one has a moral. If people respect good and follow it, they will conquer evil.

Indonesian myths come from many sources. Some are taken from Hindu writings. Others are native to the islands. Even today, myths are an important part of life in Indonesia. Dances, plays, and stories all tell these tales of good and evil.

Case Study Review

1. How can a viewer tell that Rangda is evil?
2. **Drawing Conclusions** Why do you think myths in Indonesia come from many sources?

By the early 1700s, the Dutch had taken over most of what is today Indonesia. Other European nations soon established colonies in Southeast Asia. They wanted to control the spices and raw materials available in the region.

Portuguese explorer Vasco da Gama was the first European to find an ocean route. He came to Malacca on the Malay Peninsula in 1511. The Dutch were the next important visitors. By the early 1700s, the Dutch ruled most of Indonesia.

In the late 1700s, the British gained a toehold in Southeast Asia. They founded the port of Singapore. With its convenient location, it became the busiest port in the region. The British soon had most of Malaysia under their rule.

Then countries in Europe began to build factories. They needed more and more raw materials, such as cotton and tin. **Colonies**, or the territories these European countries controlled, became a good source of these raw materials. During the 1700s and 1800s, Europeans scrambled to win control of territories around the world. They competed in Africa, India, and Southeast Asia to gain the richest sources of raw materials. They then shipped these materials to their factories in Europe.

France took over Vietnam, Cambodia, and Laos during the 1800s. The United States won the Philippines from Spain in 1898.

Part of the reason for the success of the Western powers was sheer power. They had more weapons and trained soldiers, they were organized, and they used the fact that most of the Southeast Asian countries did not get along with one another.

The Effects of Western Rule

The Western powers set up plantations to grow crops, such as rubber and tea. They built roads, railroads, schools, and hospitals. They also often kept local leaders from fighting one another.

However, the Western nations took the best land and paid little or nothing for it. They paid local workers very little. The European nations took raw materials from the colonies back to Europe. With these raw materials, they manufactured finished products. Then they brought back the products they made and sold them in the colonies. European factory-made goods sold for less money than handcrafted local goods. Local makers of cloth and other products could not compete. Many stopped making the products that they had made for centuries.

Thailand was the one place in Southeast Asia that escaped foreign rule. It did this with the help of a clever ruler, King Mongkut. He wrote that "sense and wisdom" were the only true weapons he had. He was right.

The French were in Indochina, to Thailand's east. The British were in Burma, to the west. In the early 1900s, Mongkut made treaties with both Britain and France. Thailand gave land to both countries, but kept most of its land.

On Assignment...

What events in this section are most important to put in your mini-history? Make notes and draw sketches to illustrate the pages you will include.

Section 2 Review

1. What effects did colonization have on the local economies in Southeast Asia?
2. **Drawing Conclusions** Why do you think that European powers were so eager to colonize Southeast Asia?

SECTION 3

Southeast Asians Fight for Freedom

How did Southeast Asians win their independence?

It was 1905. The Japanese army had just defeated the Russian army. It was the first time that an Asian country had defeated a European country. It was an event that inspired the nations of Southeast Asia.

The Push for Independence

During the early 1900s, Europe's Southeast Asian colonies began to agitate for independence. As in India, the people who led the struggle were often those who had been educated in European-run schools, where they had learned about freedom and democracy. They became inspired to fight for their own independence.

The Europeans had no intention of letting go, though. The one colony that managed to gain its independence was the Philippines. In 1934, the United States agreed to let the Philippines become independent in ten years. In 1946, it became the first colony in Asia to become a free country.

For the rest of the colonies, it took World War II to change things. During the war, Japan occupied most of Southeast Asia. At first, many in the region were pleased. The Japanese attack meant that the hated European powers would leave.

Then it became clear that Japanese rule was no better than European rule. The Japanese destroyed temples and killed people. They took food and supplies from Southast Asia to fight the war.

The people of the region soon began to organize against the Japanese. They received aid from the nations fighting Japan during World War II. With that money, they formed guerrilla groups to fight the Japanese. **Guerrilla warfare** is a tactic that uses hit-and-run attacks by small bands of fighters against a larger power.

After the defeat of the Japanese, the colonies pushed for their independence. The Europeans had been weakened by the wars. That helped the colonies succeed. Thus, the war helped the nations of Southeast Asia become independent.

Burma The Burmese fought the Japanese and won in 1945. The British returned to Burma after the war and tried to convince the Burmese that they again needed British rule. The Burmese did not agree. They fiercely opposed the British. In 1948, Burma became a republic.

The next decades were rocky. There were fights among different groups in Burma. For almost 30 years, a military dictator, Ne Win, controlled the country. In 1990, free elections were held and the people voted Ne Win out. His response was to take control again. His opponents were forced to leave the country or be jailed. Ne Win changed Burma's name to Myanmar.

Malaysia The push for Malaysian independence faced one big problem. The peoples who lived in Malaysia did not get along with each other. In the 1940s, only about half of the people were Malay. The Chinese population was 37 percent. The Chinese had come to Malaysia to work on plantations and to help the British build railroads. Another 12 percent of the population was Indian. In 1957, the agreement that was reached to make Malaysia a state tried to ensure that each group had power. The Malays, who

Chapter 5

were afraid that the Chinese and Indians would control the country's economy, were given a chance at more jobs.

Indonesia The Dutch were determined to keep Indonesia after World War II. The Indonesians were just as determined to gain independence. Since the early 1900s, the Indonesians had been fighting for their independence. After World War II, Indonesia declared itself a state. The Dutch fought, but in 1949, they gave up. The Indonesian will for freedom was too strong.

Indonesia was ruled by President Sukarno, a Communist, until 1966. It was a time of unrest. As early as 1959, Sukarno declared martial law to quell disturbances. There were several attempts to take over the government. A half-million people may have died in anti-Communist riots in 1965. Finally, Sukarno left office. He was replaced by President Suharto, who rejected communism and set up a democracy.

Singapore After World War II, Singapore kept its ties to Britain. Although the country became self-governing in 1959, it stayed close to Britain. In 1963, it joined with Malaya, North Borneo, and Sarawak to form Malaysia. That did not last, though. The Malays were suspicious of Singapore because of its large Chinese population. In 1965, Singapore became an independent nation.

Vietnam French rule was never accepted by the Vietnamese. In the 1920s, many called for the French to leave. In 1930, Ho Chi Minh formed a Communist party. After

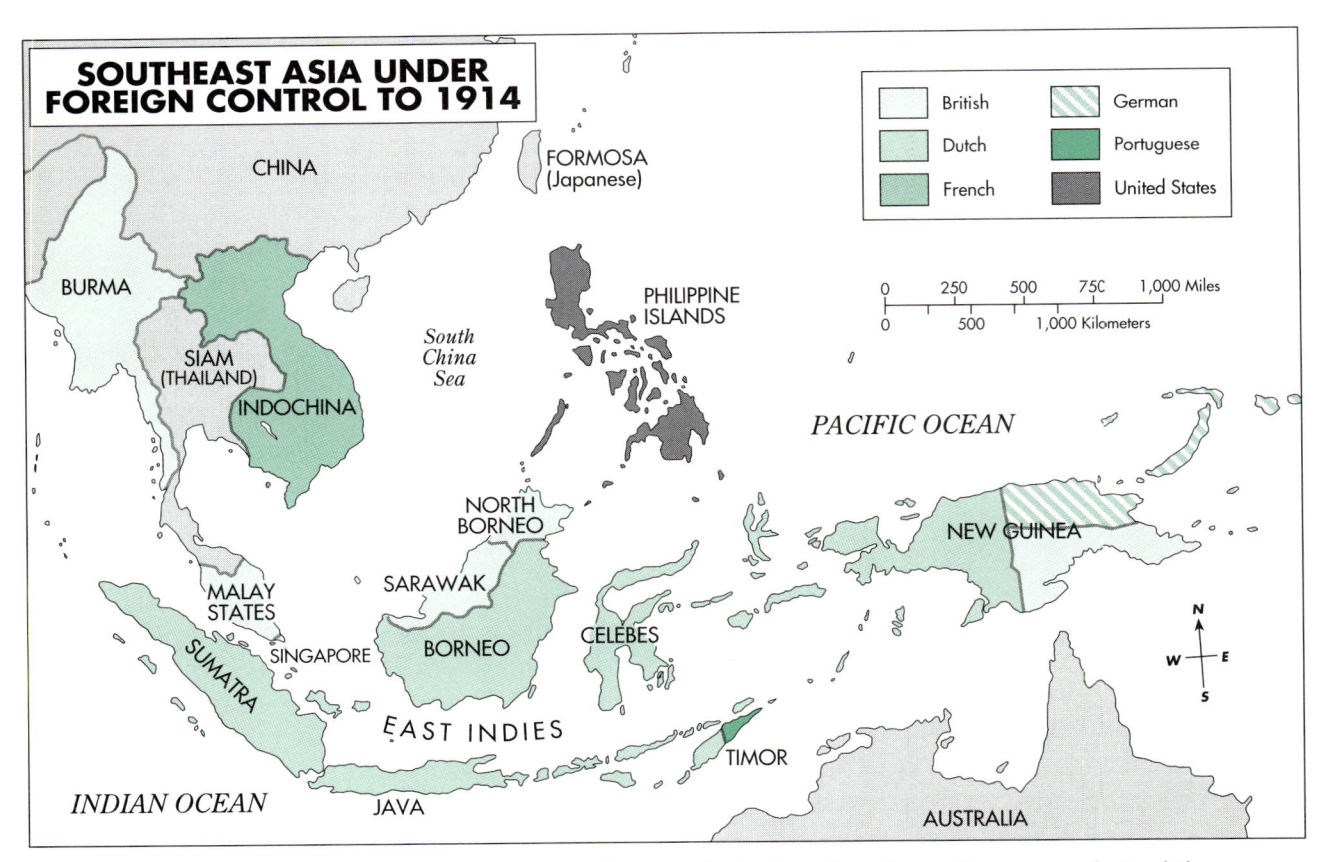

Region At first, Europeans were attracted to Southeast Asia for its spices. Later, Europeans desired the region's raw materials. Which nations claimed land in Southeast Asia?

Made up of one main island and more than 50 small islets, Singapore is Southeast Asia's leading financial center. Its location at the tip of the Malay Peninsula has made the city of Singapore an important port.

World War II, Ho Chi Minh and his party saw their chance. For eight years, they fought the French. In 1954, the French withdrew, signing an agreement that left the Communists in control of the North. The Vietnamese who supported the French would retain control over South Vietnam.

Under the terms of the agreement, Vietnam was supposed to reunite in two years. Instead, the leader of the South refused. Ngo Dinh Diem (ngaw dihn dzee•EHM) was afraid that the Communists would win control of the entire country. Diem was not popular with his own people, though. His government was corrupt and he did not improve his people's lives.

The North saw a chance to make the whole country Communist and began to wage guerrilla warfare. Then Diem was killed in a coup in 1963. Chaos followed.

The United States feared that if the Communists won, the rest of Southeast Asia would become Communist, too. This was called the domino theory. The United States then entered the war.

For more than a decade, U.S. forces joined with the South Vietnamese to fight the North Vietnamese. More than two million Vietnamese died and 57,000 U.S. soldiers were killed. It was the longest war the United States had ever fought and one of the most bitter. Many in the United States protested U.S. involvement in this war.

In January 1973, the United States and North Vietnam signed a peace agreement that soon fell apart. In 1975, the Communists gathered their forces for one last effort. They overran South Vietnam and won the war. In 1976, the country reunited; it was a Communist state.

Cambodia Neighboring Cambodia had supported South Vietnam. Then, when South Vietnam fell to the Communists, a Communist group came to power in Cambodia. This group, led by Pol Pot, murdered anyone who disagreed with it. Two to three million people, out of a population of seven million, may have died.

Pol Pot's brutality led the Vietnamese to invade Cambodia. But Pol Pot's forces fought back. Finally, in 1991, the parties signed a peace treaty.

Section 3 Review

1. Why did the United States enter the Vietnam War?
2. **Analyzing Information** How did education help create the desire for independence in Southeast Asia?

On Assignment...

Decide on one or two events from this section to include in your mini-history. Choose events that are important as well as those that might interest third graders.

REVIEWING CHAPTER 5

I. Reviewing Vocabulary

Match each word on the left with the correct definition on the right.

1. animism
2. colony
3. migrate
4. guerrilla warfare

a. a land that is controlled by another country
b. the belief that spirits live in the natural world
c. hit-and-run attacks by small bands of fighters against a larger power
d. to move from one place to another

II. Understanding the Chapter

Answer the questions below on a separate sheet of paper.

1. List and describe two ancient civilizations in Southeast Asia.
2. Why were European powers able to control Southeast Asia?
3. Why did Southeast Asia want to throw off foreign rule in the 1900s?
4. Why did the Southeast Asians first welcome the Japanese in the 1930s and 1940s? Why did they change their minds?

III. Building Skills: Understanding Chronology

Put these events in chronological order, or the order in which they occurred.

1. The Japanese take over most of Southeast Asia.
2. The Angkor kingdom is formed.
3. The United States enters the Vietnam War.
4. Vasco da Gama sails to the Malay Peninsula.
5. The Dutch colonize Indonesia.

IV. Working Together

In a small group, choose one event from this chapter and create a newspaper that explains it. Include news stories and features that show the point of view of a person who was there. Design a page that includes headlines and pictures.

On Assignment...

Creating a Mini-History: Decide on three topics to present in your mini-history. Keep in mind that your audience is third graders. Collect your mini-histories into a 10- to 12-page booklet. Present your final product to your class and to any third graders that you know.

CHAPTER 6

Changing Patterns of Life in Southeast Asia

How do most people in Southeast Asia live?

Batik is the Southeast Asian art of cloth design. Artists, like this woman in Java, Indonesia, use wax to create intricate designs on cloth. The cloth is then dyed and the wax is removed. The result is a beautiful work of wearable art.

Looking at Key Terms
- **kampung** a village
- **consensus** an agreement reached by a group as a whole or by a majority
- **incense** material that makes a scent when burned
- **gong** a round musical instrument that is struck
- **percussion instrument** a musical instrument that is played by striking it
- **gilded** covered with a thin layer of gold

On Assignment...

Giving a Presentation: In this chapter, you will write a talk for people who want to travel to Southeast Asia. In each section, think about what visitors would like to know about the region. Think about pictures that you would show the travelers. At the end of the chapter, you will assemble your notes and write your talk.

SECTION 1

Patterns of Life in Southeast Asia

How are the cultures of the people of Southeast Asia changing?

Cik rubbed his eyes. The golden sunrise had just begun to fill the Malaysian sky. It was reflected in the still water in the rice paddies. It was time to get up. Around the **kampung**, or village, he could hear a voice, a laugh. Then silence.

The children were already in the kitchen, getting ready for the walk to school. Cik's children will probably go to school through sixth grade. Only about 30 percent of the village children will have further schooling.

Cik swung his feet off his sleeping mat and lit the kerosene lamp. Then he put on his sarong, a piece of cotton cloth that he wrapped around his waist.

His wife came in from the other room. She smiled. "Rice?" she asked, giving him a bowl. Cik ate the rice and vegetables quickly. Then he took his knife from a corner. It was sharp and long, the perfect tool for cutting the weeds from the rice paddies.

Outside, the sun had cleared the horizon. Others were already at work, bent over the water. They hacked at the weeds. Growing rice is an endless job. First, the paddies are plowed with a water buffalo. Then the rice is planted. Now it was the time when the shoots are young and weeds grow everywhere. Cik waded through the water, his sarong pulled up. He was barefooted. He knew that by the time he ended his work, there would be huge leeches, bloodsucking worms, to pull off his legs. The blood I lose to those leeches, he thought, and sighed.

Throughout the morning, Cik worked on. The sun rose. Sweat shone on his back as the day became hot. Cik squinted at the sun. Soon, it would be time for the main meal of the day. He rose and stretched. Around him, he saw that his neighbors were still bent over their work. Their wide, round hats reflected the sun. Beyond the rice paddies on which Cik worked, he could see terraces of rice paddies on the mountainside. Beyond that were the hazy greens and blues of the rain forest.

Cik heard a clicking noise and looked up. To his right, walking carefully on the edge of the paddy, was a young boy with a long stick. In front of him was a family of geese. With

A Cambodian farmer drives a water buffalo across a rice field. Most farmers in Southeast Asia work the land in much the same way as their ancestors have done for many generations.

64   Chapter 6

Along the Mekong River, Cambodians take time to enjoy The Waters Feast. Part of the festivities include a boating competition. Teams paddle their canoes to compete in contests of speed and skill.

gentle clicks and swats of the stick, the boy moved the geese along. Soon, Cik thought, his children would be old enough to help him. But then there would be another problem. There was not enough land for all the children to make a living. At some point, they probably would have to leave.

Cik's life is one that millions of people in Southeast Asia understand. Two out of three people farm. Rice is the region's most important crop. Most families grow rice, and just enough vegetables to feed their family. On many of the islands of Indonesia, ash from volcanoes has left the soil rich. In some of the lowlands, rich soil washes down from the mountains during the rainy season. In much of Southeast Asia, farmers grow two or three crops of rice a year.

Village Government

Most of the kampungs in Southeast Asia are poor. Houses are made of bamboo or boards. In Malaysia, the custom is to build the houses on stilts, to protect them from flooding. In Indonesia and other countries, dirt floors are common. Many villages do not have electricity.

Government in these villages is often based on **consensus**, agreement by the group as a whole or by a majority. The people of the village choose a leader who makes decisions based on what everyone agrees to. The idea of consensus and cooperation may have come from the way in which Southeast Asians work in the rice paddies. Everyone in the village must cooperate to grow the village's rice. Perhaps that cooperation was the model for village government.

Rice is not the only crop in these rich lands. There also are rubber and tea plantations and pepper and spice farms. In villages on the coast, fishing is the main occupation.

Deep in the jungle, groups of people farm. They clear the forest, plant a crop, and when the land becomes less fertile, they move on to a new patch of land.

Festivals and Celebrations

Throughout Southeast Asia, festivals are important. In Singapore, every month brings a festival of some sort. In August, the Chinese there celebrate the Festival of the Hungry Ghosts. During that month, the dead are said to return to earth. The living entertain and feed them by putting food on their graves.

Bali, in Indonesia, is Hindu—with a twist. The Balinese have many festivals. Brightly colored flowers and food cover the temple altars. They are for the dead. But if the Balinese come back and the food is still there, they eat it. The dead must not have been hungry, they reason.

In Thailand, in April, the new year's festival of Songkran is celebrated. Children pour scented water into their parents' hands as a sign of respect. On the last day of the festival, the water pouring increases. People roam the streets, looking for people to throw water on. Luckily, it's often unbearably hot in April.

Malaysia's Chinese celebrate Chap Goh Mei in January. It's the end of the holiday season, the 15th day after the Chinese New Year. In the past, women who wished to marry went to the sea. There, they threw in oranges and wished for husbands. Often they got their wish. Waiting by the river were the young men of the village, dressed up and eager to marry.

These celebrations help to create a strong sense of community in the cultures of Southeast Asia. They remind people of their heritage and bring families together.

Family Life

For most Southeast Asians, the family is everything. In much of the Southeast Asian countryside, children live with their parents until they marry.

As part of this culture, most Southeast Asians would not think of doing things alone. The idea of moving to another part of the country for the sake of making one's own way is unknown. If people have to leave—to go to the city and make a living, for example—they are likely to live with relatives in the city. They are also likely to return home whenever they can.

Education

Today, most children in Southeast Asia go to elementary school. Some drop out to help their families farm. Others drop out because their families do not have the money for books. In some countries, schools are tied to religion. Islamic countries, such as Malaysia and Indonesia, have Muslim schools. Boys in Buddhist Vietnam often go to Buddhist schools. It is traditional in many countries for children to wear uniforms to school. Discipline tends to be strict. Students usually sit in rows and recite their lessons by heart.

Only a few fortunate students go on to high school and college. One exception is Vietnam. In the early 1990s, almost 40 percent of its people went on to high school. About 130,000 students attend college classes.

In many countries, competition for spots in high schools and colleges is intense. In some countries, such as Singapore, students who want to continue their education have to pass difficult tests.

Life for Women in Southeast Asia

Fewer girls than boys go to school. Some parents—especially those in rural areas—think that it is not important for girls to have a formal education. They believe that it is more important for a girl to learn the work of the house.

Life for women in Southeast Asia offers more freedom than life in other parts of Asia. In the Islamic countries of Malaysia and Indonesia, women have more choices than do women in other Islamic countries. In many Islamic countries, women remain veiled and in the house. In Southeast Asia, many Muslim women do not even wear a head covering. Although there are fewer chances for women to work than there are for men, many do work outside the home. In Singapore, women are expected to continue to work at paying jobs after they marry.

On Assignment...

What would travelers to Southeast Asia want to know about the region? Think what you have learned in this section that might be helpful to them. What pictures would you show?

Section 1 Review

1. Explain how most villages are governed.
2. **Drawing Conclusions** Why do you think that education is more valued in the cities than it is in the country?

SECTION 2

Arts and Literature in Southeast Asia

What is unique about the arts and literature in Southeast Asia?

It is about 9 P.M. in the village. The people sit on folding chairs. In the front of the auditorium, a sheet hangs down. On a pole in one corner is a bull's skull. There is a burning stick of **incense** in the top of the skull. Beside the sheet is a group of men with **gongs** and other instruments. The light dims in the auditorium. The people grow quiet. A man dressed in white walks down the center aisle. He is carrying a lit torch and a handful of shadow puppets. The puppets are made of tooled leather. The man, called the *dalang*, takes his place behind the sheet. The torchlight flickers, throwing light on the sheet.

Soon, the dalang begins the *wayang kulit*, or shadow play. In a singsong voice, he tells the story. He plays the parts of all the characters. The puppets' lacy shadows dance across the sheet. The plays are usually ancient Hindu epics. For hundreds of years, Indonesians have enjoyed the retellings of these tales.

The dalang's voice chants on. For at least six hours, he will recite the story by heart, moving the puppets and saying their parts. The dalang is a scholar, a priest, and a holy man. The musicians play their instruments. The audience members come and go. The hypnotic voice of the dalang continues until dawn.

The elements of the wayang kulit show some of the reasons that the arts of Southeast Asia fascinate others. They are based on fantasy, religion, and mystery. They are colorful and almost otherworldly. Princes, demon monkeys, gods, and witches all play a part in the arts of Southeast Asia.

Vietnamese water puppets are another unique art form. These puppets appear to be floating on water. The puppeteers control the puppets from elsewhere.

In Southeast Asia, religion takes on a different feeling than it does in other places in the world. The people of Southeast Asia have taken the major religions of the world and fit them to their lives—and their arts. The wayang kulit is one example. Indonesia is 90 percent Muslim, but the popular wayang plays are based on Hindu stories. In the Philippines, the *cenaculo* is a play based on the life of Jesus Christ. This play, with its bright masks and fancy costumes, is a version that you would only see in the Philippines.

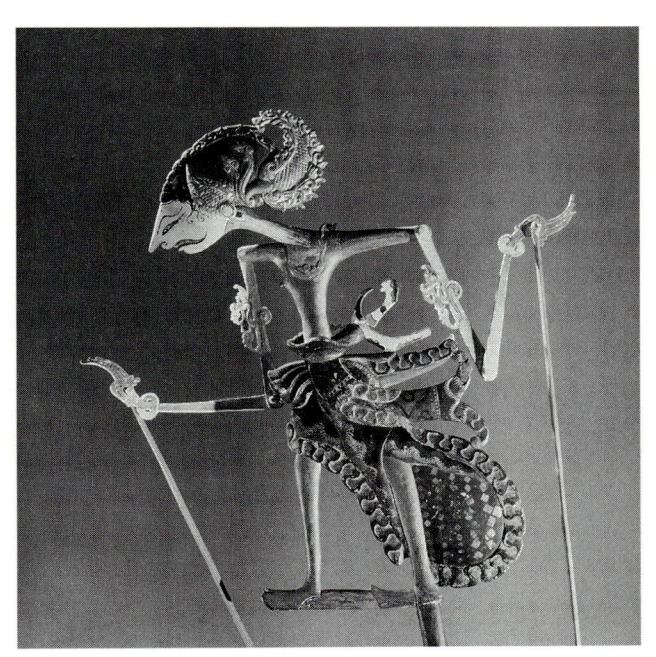

Shadow puppets are operated by a skilled dalang. The puppets retell the stories of ancient Hindu epics.

Many of Southeast Asia's arts were influenced by the cultures of India and China. Hindu and Buddhist epics and stories from India and China are the basis for many of the best-loved plays, poems, and stories in Southeast Asia.

Music The Indonesian gamelan orchestra is another strong tradition in Southeast Asia. The gamelan orchestra is at least 1,000 years old. It is made up of gongs and instruments like xylophones. Other **percussion instruments** round out the orchestra. The gamelan can sound like rippling water or like crashing waves. One thing is certain. It sounds quite different from Western music. Gamelan music is played for puppet shows and for religious rituals. It also accompanies dances.

Other Southeast Asian cultures have similar musical styles. For example, in the Philippines, the kulintang, a set of gongs, is popular. Like the music of the gamelan, music from the kulintang has a haunting quality.

Dance Most Westerners have seen photographs of the beautiful dances of Southeast Asia. The women often wear heavy **gilded** headdresses, which are covered with a thin layer of gold. Their clothes are made of silk and gold. They use tiny, graceful movements to tell a story. Often, the story is an ancient tale from Hindu legend. Sometimes it is a dance to help the rains come or to drive away evil spirits. In Thailand, the fingernail dance is popular. It was developed by wealthy women of ancient days who did not have to work. They could afford to allow their fingernails to grow very long. They then used these unusual fingernails as the basis for the dance.

Literature For many generations, the literature of Southeast Asia was an oral tradition that was handed down from parents to their children. Some stories were based on religious epics. Others were fantastic tales of heroism and love. In recent years, modern writers have begun to have these and other stories printed. In the early 1900s in the Philippines, José Rizal wrote about his country's wish for freedom.

On Assignment...
What information from this section would a traveler want to know? What pictures could illustrate what you want to say?

Art and Architecture Southeast Asia's art and architecture is also unique. In Thailand, golden temples with tall spires reach the sky. The ancient Buddhas of Indonesia's Borobodur gaze silently at visitors.

Other ancient arts are still practiced. The art of batik was invented in Southeast Asia. Artists paint tiny areas of cloth with wax. Then they dye the cloth. The process is repeated many times. Some batiks can take six months or more to finish. In the old royal courts of Indonesia, certain patterns and colors were only for the king and his family. Today, anyone can buy the more than 1,000 designs.

Section 2 Review

1. How has religion influenced the arts in Southeast Asia?
2. **Identifying Relationships** How are the arts of different countries in Southeast Asia similar?

Case Study 6

Preserving a Great Heritage: The Ancient Capital of Angkor

If you look at the Cambodian flag, you will find something very special—the towers of Angkor Wat, the largest religious structure in the world. To modern Cambodians, the great building symbolizes pride in their past. It represents the hope that they, like their ancestors, can build a strong nation.

From the 1100s to the 1400s, the ancient Khymer empire ruled over present-day Cambodia, as well as parts of Vietnam, Laos, and Thailand. Its capital Angkor bustled with soldiers, citizens, monks, and traders. Royal buildings covered more than three times the space covered by Manhattan Island.

The largest monument was Angkor Wat, or "temple of the capital." Its design represents the home of the Hindu gods. The five towers represent the peaks of sacred mountains. The outer walls symbolize the world's edge. The moat surrounding the temple stands for the sea. Carvings of demons, serpents, gods, and kings tell stories of heavenly and earthly history.

Although Angkor was abandoned in the 1400s, the Cambodian people have worked quietly to preserve their heritage. Today, citizens like Uong Von, a government official, volunteer to clear vines and to sweep the sacred sites. If you visited the ancient capital city, you would see little old women pulling weeds and young men cutting brush with huge knives. They are not paid, but they believe that it is the right thing to do.

The nations of the world have also recognized the value of preserving the ancient buildings. International help may mean that Angkor will be rebuilt. Until then, the Cambodian people will volunteer to clear rubble and restore statues. No matter what happens, Angkor will remain a lasting monument to the Khymer civilization. And the huge stone war elephants and ancient gods will stand watch for many more centuries.

Case Study Review

1. Explain what a visitor to ancient Angkor would find most amazing.
2. **Analyzing Information** Why do you think other nations are interested in preserving Angkor?

REVIEWING CHAPTER 6

I. Reviewing Vocabulary

Match each word on the left with the correct definition on the right.

1. consensus
2. gong
3. kampung
4. gilded

a. a village
b. an agreement reached by a group as a whole or by a majority
c. covered with a thin layer of gold
d. a round musical instrument that is struck

II. Understanding the Chapter

Answer the questions below on a separate sheet of paper.

1. How is village life changing in Southeast Asia?
2. Describe the role of the family in the life of Southeast Asians.
3. Describe what life is like for women in Southeast Asia.
4. How did China and India influence the arts of Southeast Asia?

III. Building Skills: Distinguishing Fact From Opinion

Look at the statements below. Decide which are facts and which are opinions. Explain your choices.

1. Many people in Southeast Asian villages grow rice.
2. Women have a better life in Southeast Asia than they do in the Middle East.
3. The festivals of Southeast Asia are exciting.
4. Only within the last century has there been much written literature in Southeast Asia.

IV. Working Together

Split up into six groups. Find five words from the chapter that are new to all of you. Write these words on separate pieces of paper. Put your pieces of paper into a box with the papers of the other groups. Take turns drawing pieces of paper and defining the words.

On Assignment...

Giving a Presentation: Review your notes from this chapter. Think about the audience who will listen to your talk. What will these people want to know about traveling to Southeast Asia? What pictures will illustrate your information? Write a three-minute talk. When you have finished, practice it with a friend. Have your friend make suggestions for improving your talk. Then revise it and present the travel talk to your class.

CHAPTER 7

Southeast Asia in the World Today

What forces are shaping Southeast Asia in the modern world?

Stores selling televisions, video recorders, computers, and other electronic items appear all over Southeast Asia. As the economy improves, more people are able to afford such luxuries.

Looking at Key Terms

- **capitalism** an economic system in which businesses are owned privately
- **market economy** a system in which prices are based on what people are willing to pay and companies make goods based on what people want to buy
- **insecticide** a chemical that kills insects
- **rigid** stiff; tightly controlled
- **investors** people who put money into businesses in hopes of making a profit

On Assignment...

Creating a Board Game: In this chapter, you will learn about Southeast Asia in today's world. You will then use this information to write questions for a game. In each section, you will write questions about what you learned. At the end of the chapter, you will design a board game that uses these questions. Then you can play the game.

SECTION 1

The Economy of Southeast Asia

What are some recent economic trends in Southeast Asia?

The young woman bends to her task. The black glasses keep out the glare of the welding light. She holds the torch with ease. The glare of white light highlights the bicycle frame that she is welding.

There will always be a market for the bicycles Doan Nga is making. Behind her are piles of finished bicycles. The tools seem old. The workers have to cross the street to paint the bicycles.

"It is a state-owned factory," Doan says on her lunch break. "We have to make 16,000 bicycles a year." She shrugs. "If this factory were arranged better, we could make many more. But we have our goal. We meet it."

In Vietnam, as in some other Southeast Asian countries, Communist nations are struggling to incorporate **capitalism** to help their economies. Capitalism is an economic system in which businesses are owned privately. In Vietnam, people are now allowed to own businesses. Like this bicycle factory, though, many businesses are still owned by the state.

Challenges of Independence

When the colonies of Southeast Asia became independent after World War II, they faced a number of challenges. Before independence, Westerners owned and ran the businesses. The Western powers saw Southeast Asia as a place that supplied metals, lumber, and rice. Those products left the colonies. Finished goods were imported.

When the Western powers left, there was little industry in the former colonies. The newly independent nations needed to build new industries, but this was difficult. For one thing, there was little money for factories. Also, many of those who knew how to run factories were Westerners, and they were gone.

COUNTRIES OF SOUTHEAST ASIA

COUNTRY	CAPITAL CITY	AREA (square miles)	POPULATION (millions of people)	POPULATION DOUBLING TIME (years)
Brunei	Bandar Seri Begawan	2,030	0.3	27
Cambodia	Phnom Penh	68,150	9.0	27
Indonesia	Jakarta	705,190	187.6	42
Laos	Viangchan	89,110	4.6	24
Malaysia	Kuala Lumpur	126,850	18.4	30
Myanmar	Yangon	253,880	43.5	36
Philippines	Manila	115,120	64.6	28
Singapore	Singapore	240	2.8	55
Thailand	Bangkok	197,250	57.2	49
Vietnam	Hanoi	125,670	71.8	31

Source: World Population Data Sheet of the Population Reference Bureau, Inc.

The countries of Southeast Asia vary greatly in size and population. Which country is smallest in size? Which is largest? Which country has the most people? In how many years will this country's population double?

Southeast Asian countries dealt with these problems in different ways. Some adopted communism. Communist countries such as Cambodia, Laos, and Vietnam set up economies in which the state owned the factories. This helped countries to build new factories quickly. It also led to a system in which factories could make more of a product than people wanted to buy. Like the bicycle factory in which Doan Nga works, state-owned businesses did not need to use the most efficient methods of making products because they had no worries about profits—or losses.

States such as Thailand and the Philippines set up **market economies**. In a market economy, private companies own and run the businesses. Privately owned companies decide how much of a product to make based on the demand for that product.

In a market economy, business owners risk losing their money and their business if they do not pay careful attention to the needs of their customers and to their methods of manufacturing. A number of Southeast Asian countries blend communism and market economics. Indonesia is one of these. For instance, the government owns Pertamina, the country's oil company. Many smaller companies are owned and run by individual Indonesians, though.

In recent years, many Communist countries have been trying to change. Communism has proved to be an inefficient system for running industries.

Singapore: A Southeast Asian Jewel

Singapore is one of Southeast Asia's success stories. Led for almost four decades by Lee Kuan Yew, the country has prospered.

Singapore was also known as a place where people were fined for littering. Often, those who disagreed with Lee were jailed. But Singapore became a very good place to do business. Its people were well educated. It welcomed money from people in other countries who wanted to start companies. All this made Singapore's economy soar.

Southeast Asian governments include military dictatorships, Communist governments, constitutional monarchies, and democracies. Outside the royal palace in Phnom Penh, Cambodia, a crowd carries pictures of Prince Norodom Sihanouk.

This country, which is about the size of Chicago, has the second-highest living standard in Asia. That means its people live well. There is little unemployment. Many people work in factories. The country is also known for its busy port. Tourists are eager to visit because the country is known for being clean and safe. All this makes Singapore a jewel in the crown of Southeast Asia.

What Singapore doesn't have is land. That lack of farmland means that Singapore is very different from the rest of Southeast Asia, where more than 50 percent of the people make a living by farming.

Chapter 7

Buses and motorcycles jockey for position on a crowded street in Bangkok, Thailand. Like other cities in Southeast Asia, Bangkok has experienced tremendous growth since the 1950s.

Agriculture

Farming is changing in Southeast Asia, too. In the 1950s and 1960s, farmers began to grow new kinds of rice. They began to use chemicals to help them farm. As a result, they were able to grow much more food. Countries had to import less rice. There was less hunger. All these changes created a phenomenon called the *Green Revolution*.

The Green Revolution also meant that many farmers had to borrow money for chemicals and equipment to increase their crop yield.

If farmers had a bad year and couldn't pay their loans, they lost their farms. Farmers began to grow crops other than rice. Coffee, rubber, and tobacco were grown on land that families once used only for rice.

The Green Revolution had environmental effects. The chemicals that farmers used began to show up in the water supply. Farmers no longer grew many kinds of rice. If a disease or pest attacked one kind of rice, the crop was in trouble across an entire country. In Java, an island in Indonesia, the brown planthopper, a bug that had not been a problem before, killed rice crops across the island. Planthoppers liked the new kind of rice.

Farmers began to realize that the **insecticides** that they had sprayed to get rid of pests could cause additional problems. These insecticides had killed the animals that ate the planthoppers. As a result, Indonesia banned some insecticides. It also tried to plant different kinds of rice.

Moving to the Cities

Even though most people in Southeast Asia still farm, more and more people are moving to the cities. In Bangkok, for example, there were one million people in 1950. By the mid-1990s, there were over seven million.

People come to the city because there is no more farmland and because they want better jobs. When they get to the cities, many live in shacks with no electricity, running water, or plumbing. Even so, these people can often make more money in cities than they can make at home. In the rural northeast of Thailand, almost half the income of the people comes from Bangkok. Why? Family members who live there send money home to relatives in the country.

Those who come to the city often live with friends and relatives who are already there. The result is a series of small cities-within-cities that contain people from the same area in the country. These people live together and often help one another find jobs.

There are other people, however, like many of those in Singapore, who live much better lives in the cities. They have good jobs

> **On Assignment...**
>
> Create some questions for your game about Southeast Asia today. Write your questions and answers on a piece of paper. Make sure that your questions cover the most important facts you learned in this section.

and cars. They have money for movies and eating out. In some cities, such as Jakarta, a visitor can see many middle-class people.

But beyond their well-kept houses and apartments, there is another Jakarta. It is a land of dirt roads and families jammed together in shacks. It is a world of little work, of illness, and of dirty water.

Section 1 Review

1. How has farming in Southeast Asia changed as a result of the Green Revolution? What problems did the Green Revolution cause?
2. **Making a Chart** Make a chart that shows the differences between market economies and Communist economies.

SECTION 2

Political Trends in Southeast Asia

How are the governments of Southeast Asia changing?

Like Great Britain, Thailand is a constitutional monarchy. As you read in the Introduction, a constitutional monarchy allows the king and queen only limited power. In Vietnam, communism is still strong. In Singapore, leaders are elected—but there is only one real political party.

The countries of Southeast Asia have many different kinds of governments. Everyone from kings to Communists reigns. Nowhere is there a democracy as free as that of the United States, however.

Southeast Asia has faced many problems in its search for stable government. As you saw in Section 1, after World War II, newly independent countries had to build their own economies when the Western powers left. Then the war in Indochina dragged on for decades. The war unsettled many countries and made some armies too strong.

Vietnam and Laos are Communist countries. Communism as a form of government is becoming rarer in the world. The Soviet Union was once a huge Communist state. Its fall, in 1991, shook Communists around the world. Cambodia, which had been Communist, voted in 1993 to have a king rule. In Vietnam, more and more private businesses are allowed. Communist rule is

In Myanmar, Daw Aung San Suu Kyi speaks out against the military government. In 1991, she was awarded the Nobel Peace Prize.

becoming less common, as well as less **rigid**, or tightly controlled.

Military control has also been a factor in Southeast Asian governments. Some countries, such as Myanmar, or Burma, are still under army rule. Myanmar's people are not allowed to vote and military leaders are all-powerful.

In other countries, there is a strong military voice in government. One example is Indonesia. In Indonesia, there are elections with several political parties, but only one really counts. That party is supported by the army.

Challenge and Change in the Philippines

The story of power in the Philippines shows how progress can be made against a leader who rules with the support of the army. Ferdinand Marcos became president of the Philippines in 1965. He ruled with an iron hand. He gave his friends big jobs and he looted the country for himself.

The people of the Philippines showed their anger at this corruption in 1972. They began to protest. Marcos then declared martial law. He jailed many political enemies.

His biggest opponent was Benigno Aquino. Marcos put him in jail. In 1980, Marcos allowed Aquino to go to the United States. In 1983, Marcos's wife warned Aquino not to return to the Philippines. "You may be killed," she said.

She was right. When Aquino returned to the Philippines, he was shot and killed. The country was outraged. Many thought that Marcos had had Aquino killed. People across the country protested.

In 1986, Marcos called for elections. Aquino's widow, Corazon, decided to run against Marcos. After the election, Marcos declared victory. The election was clearly rigged, though. The people rose up. There were rallies everywhere for "people power" and for Corazon Aquino. The Catholic Church backed the movement. Even the army would not support Marcos.

On Assignment...

Write at least five questions about the information in this section for your board game. Write some questions about the political trends you studied.

Finally, Marcos fled to Hawaii. For the people of the Philippines, it was a moment of triumph. It showed that people power can be stronger than dictatorship.

Aquino took power and brought democracy to the Philippines. She faced big problems, though. Most Filipinos are poor. Aquino faced coups by Marcos supporters in the army. She won those fights. She also faced a movement by Muslims in the Philippines who wanted their own country. In 1992, she stepped down. The people elected Fidel Ramos, whom she supported. Corazon Aquino's story proved one thing to the people of the Philippines. They had the ability, and the right, to rid their country of a dictator.

Section 2 Review

1. What are the main types of governments in Southeast Asia?
2. **Analyzing Information** Why do you think that the Filipinos were able to force Marcos out?

SECTION 3

Southeast Asia and the World

How is Southeast Asia's role in the world changing?

Until World War II, many Westerners thought of Southeast Asia as a place to buy resources such as rice, tin, and rubber.

After World War II, however, colonies became countries. They wanted to be more than just a source for tin. They wanted to develop their own industries and to claim a place in the world economy.

Southeast Asia did have some advantages. People from other countries did not have to make big investments to start companies there. Southeast Asian workers were paid less than workers in other places. The presence of natural resources meant that the materials industries needed could be found nearby. Southeast Asia is also in a good geographic position. It links India and the Middle East with China.

Southeast Asia did have some difficulties in encouraging outside investment. World War II had left countries shattered. Many Westerners thought that their governments were not stable. In addition, until the 1980s, the Communist countries dealt mostly with other Communist countries.

In the 1970s, money began to flow into Southeast Asia. Big corporations built factories. Clothes sold in U.S. stores began to carry tags reading "Made in the Philippines" or "Made in Indonesia." But while these tags indicate that clothes are made in Southeast Asia, the company is often based in another country. The company's profits, then, do not go to Southeast Asia.

Japan is one country that is involved in the economy of Southeast Asia. Japan imports raw materials from the region. It owns plants in Southeast Asia that make goods that are sold in other parts of the world.

The Communist countries of Vietnam and Laos are beginning to welcome **investors**, or people who put money into businesses. For example, because Cambodia has become a kingdom and is no longer a Communist country, it expects more economic activity. Investors will be more willing to come to Cambodia because they can expect to make a profit.

In some ways, though, Southeast Asia is still tied to its colonial past. Other countries hold economic power there. At least now, though, Southeast Asia keeps some of that money at home.

Politics: Southeast Asia and the West

In 1967, five Southeast Asian countries united for the first time to form the Association of Southeast Asian Nations (ASEAN). This organization included Indonesia, Thailand, Malaysia, Singapore, and the Philippines. Brunei joined in 1984. ASEAN's goal is to increase trade among

Low start-up and labor costs have led many industrialized countries to build factories in Southeast Asia, like this one in Indonesia. If you check the labels on your clothing, chances are you'll find that at least one item was made in Southeast Asia.

Chapter 7

During Pol Pot's reign of terror, hundreds of thousands of Cambodians were relocated, tortured, and murdered. Thousands fled and became refugees in Thailand and many other countries throughout Southeast Asia and the world.

member nations. It also encourages members to stand together against outsiders.

ASEAN was pro-Western. That is, it was friendly toward countries like the United States. It was against the Communist movements in Southeast Asia. The United States supported ASEAN, sending money to arm the ASEAN countries against communism.

Today communism has less power because of the fall of the Communist Soviet Union. Russia no longer needs to keep its influence strong by helping Communist countries. In July 1995, what was once unthinkable happened. Vietnam joined ASEAN. The same year, Vietnam was finally recognized by the United States. Both of these links show how much the world has changed.

Since the Vietnam War—the only war the United States has ever lost—the United States has mostly stayed out of the region. For the first time in a century, there are no United States military bases in Southeast Asia. Its bases in the Philippines closed in 1992. One result of U.S. withdrawal is that Southeast Asia no longer has the nearby help of the United States.

Today, what interests the Southeast Asian countries most is China. This country of 1.2 billion people dominates Southeast Asia. The countries of Southeast Asia watch China carefully. There are still fights over some Southeast Asian islands. China says that it owns them. Other countries say that they do.

Southeast Asia, though, is developing into a worldwide economic force. It needs outside countries less. Many Southeast Asian countries have experienced strong economic growth. Southeast Asia has been a land of terrible war and of stunning beauty. Today Southeast Asia has a bright future.

On Assignment...

What information in this section could you add to your board game? Review the material and note details about Southeast Asia's economic growth. Write questions—and answers—about this information for your game.

Section 3 Review

1. What is ASEAN?
2. **Drawing Conclusions** Explain how the changes in Communist Southeast Asian countries may affect the region in the future.

Case Study 7

Return to the Killing Fields

Sarat turned her dull eyes to the interviewer. "I watched my husband die. Then my son. Do you know of Pol Pot–the leader of the Cambodian Communists? His people rounded up the people. Some they killed. They killed my husband, right in front of me. They beat him to death with sticks. He was asking 'Why? Why?' He had the wrong ideas, they said. So they killed him."

These are the killing fields, the interviewer thought.

"One day, they came and said we were going to farm," Sarat said. "We marched for days. When we got there, we began working. From day to night, we worked. They would throw down a can of rice–oh, six inches high. That would be all 10 people got all day. We starved. People ate rats. They pulled up every piece of green and ate it. That was when I had to watch my son die in my arms. He was so weak and thin that he couldn't hold his head up. He just lay there, limp.

"That work went on for four years. Of the 150 who had come, 20 were still alive. Then the Vietnamese came. We had been told that they were even worse than Pol Pot's men. So I escaped. So many others were escaping that we went with them.

"Finally, we arrived at the border of Thailand. Someone saw us and said, 'Are you refugees? Do you want to go to the camp?' We have been there since. It is not as bad as Pol Pot, but still...

"I wake in the night with dreams of my son dying in my arms. I have little to do here but think. That is something I do not want to do. Then, too, we are often hungry. People go to the woods to dig for roots to eat with the rice.

"Now you tell us we will go home. Where is home? It is 1992. My family is dead. What will I do?" Sarat buried her face in her hands.

The interviewer said, "Didn't you begin the school for the deaf children? Refugees are coming back now that Cambodia is a kingdom again. Many children are deaf from the war. Here," the man said. He scribbled some words on a piece of paper. "This is the name of a woman in Phnom Penh. She runs services for children. Good luck." It was a small hope. But it was all Sarat had.

Case Study Review

1. Describe Sarat's journey after Pol Pot took power in Cambodia.
2. **Making Inferences** Why do you think that Cambodia was called *the killing fields*?

REVIEWING CHAPTER 7

I. Reviewing Vocabulary

Match each word on the left with the correct definition on the right.

1. market economy
2. insecticide
3. capitalism
4. rigid

a. an economic system in which businesses are privately owned
b. a chemical that kills insects
c. a system in which prices are set by what people are willing to pay and companies make goods based on what people want to buy
d. stiff; tightly controlled

II. Understanding the Chapter

Answer the questions below on a separate sheet of paper.

1. Describe the different kinds of economic systems in Southeast Asia today.
2. Why do people in Southeast Asia move to the cities?
3. How did the downfall of the Soviet Union affect Vietnam?
4. Why did Cambodian refugees begin to return to their country in 1991?

III. Building Skills: Summarizing

Write a sentence that summarizes the important points about each topic below.

1. agriculture in Southeast Asia since the 1950s
2. forms of government in Southeast Asia since World War II
3. the importance of ASEAN to Southeast Asia

IV. Working Together

Work with a partner and choose one of the people you read about in this chapter. Write interview questions that you would ask this leader about his or her country and about Southeast Asia in general. Then answer your questions. Perform your interview for the class.

On Assignment...

Creating a Board Game: Organize the questions you wrote as you read this chapter. Choose the best of them to use for your game. Now create a board game based on these questions. You could create a game in which players move forward when they answer correctly. You could create a game in which falling on a certain square means that players have to answer a question. After you have designed your game, create the pieces. Now practice playing it to make sure that it works.

CHAPTER 8

Australia, New Zealand, and Oceania

What do Australia, New Zealand, and Oceania have in common? How are they different?

Australia is a country of contrasts. Modern cities, such as Sydney, dot the coastline. In the center of the country, small towns and villages are scattered across a rugged land.

Looking at Key Terms

- **outback** the dry lands of Australia where there are few settlers
- **geyser** a natural spring of hot water that shoots steam or hot water into the air from time to time
- **geothermal energy** energy produced from heat within the earth
- **penal colony** a colony for prisoners
- **squatter** someone who settles on land without the right to do so
- **atoll** a small coral island with a body of water at its center; most often found in the South Pacific

On Assignment...

Creating Posters: In this chapter, you will learn about Australia, New Zealand, and Oceania. Your assignment is to create two posters that will interest tourists in this part of the world. In each section, make notes about what tourists should know about this region. Look for hint boxes. They contain suggestions that will give you ideas for your notes.

SECTION 1

The Land and People of Australia and New Zealand

How has geography affected where and how people live in Australia and New Zealand?

Centuries ago, Europeans thought that Australia and New Zealand were located at the end of the world. On maps it was called *Terra Australis Incognita,* which means "the unknown land to the south." England thought so little of Australia that it sent its convicts there.

All that was long ago, however. Today, Australia and New Zealand are modern countries with thriving economies. Most people there are middle class. These countries are among the most popular tourist spots on earth. In this chapter, you will find out how Australia and New Zealand went from being "unknown lands in the south" to popular tourist spots. First, however, you will read about the region's geography.

The Land, Climate, and Natural Resources of Australia

Look at the map of Australia on page 83. Australia is the world's largest island. It is also the world's smallest continent. Australia is almost as big as mainland United States. Yet in 1994, only 17.8 million people lived there. More than 259 million people called the United States home in the same year.

Physical Regions Why does Australia have so few people? One reason is the huge desert in the island's interior. One third of the country is desert, called the **outback** by Australians. Another third is semi-desert. Australia is the driest continent in the world. It is also the world's flattest continent. Its highest point is Mt. Kosciusko, which is 7,316 feet (2,230 m) high.

This island has a group of animals found nowhere else in the world. Australia is the only natural home of the kangaroo and koala bear. In fact, Australia was so isolated that it developed many species of plants and animals that are unique.

Australia has three main areas. The Great Western Plateau takes up more than half of the country. It is a dry land. At its edge, in the middle of the country, is Ayers Rock. This reddish rock is 1,000 feet (305 m) high and six miles (9.75 km) around. It is the largest rock in the world.

To the east of the Great Western Plateau lie the east-central lowlands. On Australia's eastern edge is the Great Dividing Range. This is where Mt. Kosciusko is. The Great Dividing Range drops to the eastern coastal plains, which are only 248 miles (400 km) at their widest. Even so, the plains contain the country's largest cities and are home to almost all of Australia's population.

Climate and Resources Australia is a warm country. The coldest parts are the island of Tasmania and the highlands in the southeast. There, snow sometimes falls. During the winter months in the southern hemisphere—June, July, and August—people go skiing. In the southern hemisphere, the seasons are the opposite of the seasons in the northern hemisphere. January and February are the warmest months in Australia. In the far north, closest to the equator, it is hot throughout the year.

Rain is what makes the difference in Australia. The Great Dividing Range stops the moist air from the Pacific Ocean. It falls as rain on the coastal range, where most farming takes place. In most of the rest of the country, rain is not common. When rain does come, it floods the land. Then it dries, and the land is parched again.

This dryness means that farming is hard, except along the east coast. Australia's great river system, the Murray, helps to irrigate some land in the southeast.

Sugar cane and wheat are the main crops. In most of the interior, farmers raise cattle and sheep. Australia is the world's largest producer of wool.

AUSTRALIA, NEW ZEALAND, AND OCEANIA

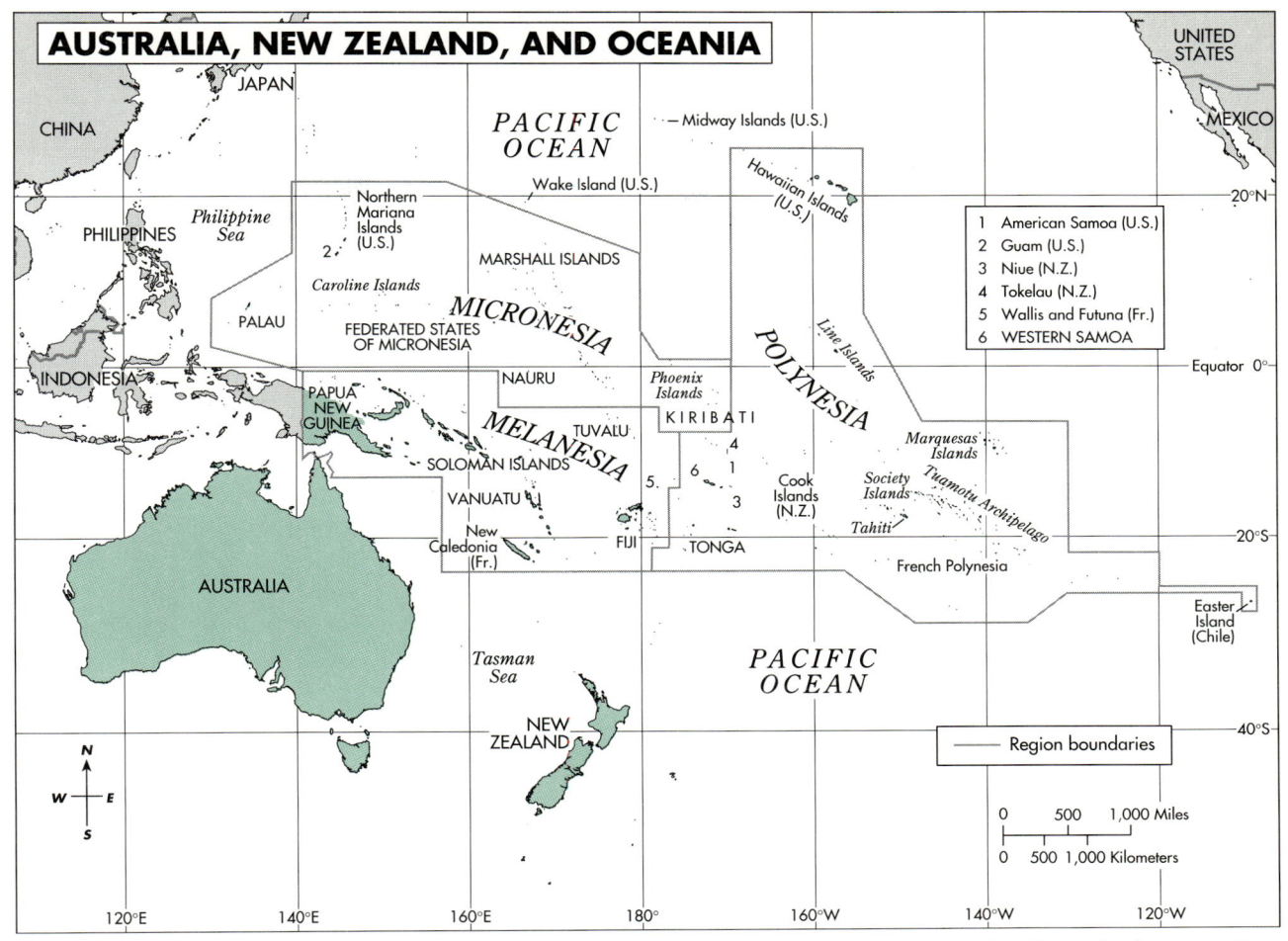

Place and Region Thousands of islands dot the Pacific Ocean. Australia and New Zealand are the largest of these islands. Into what three main groups is Oceania divided? To which group does Fiji belong?

Australia also is rich in minerals. It contains deposits of iron ore, bauxite (to make aluminum), and uranium. Australia has coal, oil, and natural gas. In the 1850s and 1880s, news of gold brought many to Australia to try to strike it rich.

The Land, Climate, and Natural Resources of New Zealand

Australia and New Zealand look quite different from one another. New Zealand is green and mountainous. As you can see on the map above, New Zealand consists mainly of two islands: North Island and South Island.

South Island has high mountains that seem to dive into deep lakes. North Island is home to 70 percent of New Zealand's people. Most of the population lives there for several reasons. North Island is warmer and has a higher annual rainfall. Its mountains are gentler. It also has the country's best farmland. As in Australia, the centers of the islands are less populated. Most New Zealanders live in cities on the coasts. The center of North Island has two active volcanoes. It also has geysers and hot springs. **Geysers** are springs of hot water that gush into the air.

To some, New Zealand seems to have an ideal climate. It rains regularly. Summers are

Chapter 8

SOME FACTS ABOUT AUSTRALIA, NEW ZEALAND, AND OCEANIA

COUNTRY	CAPITAL	AREA (square miles)	POPULATION (millions of people)	RESOURCES AND MAJOR INDUSTRIES
Australia	Canberra	2,941,290	17.8	wheat, barley, oats, coal, copper, iron, steel, textiles
Fiji	Suva	7,050	0.8	sugar, bananas, gold, timber, tourism
French Polynesia	Papette	1,410	0.2	coconuts, bananas, sugar, tourism
Marshall Islands	Majuro	70	0.05	agriculture, tourism
Micronesia	Palikir	271	0.1	tropical fruits, vegetables, coconuts
New Caledonia	Noumea	7,060	0.2	nickel, chrome, iron, cobalt, manganese, silver, gold, lead, copper
New Zealand	Wellington	103,470	3.4	grains, fruits, oil, gas, iron, coal, food processing, textiles, wool, timber
Papua New Guinea	Port Moresby	174,850	3.9	coffee, coconuts, cocoa, gold, copper, silver
Solomon Islands	Honiara	10,810	0.3	coconuts, rice, bananas, yams, fish canning
Vanuatu	Port-Vila	4,710	0.2	copra, cocoa, coffee, manganese, fish-freezing, meat canneries, tourism
Western Samoa	Apia	1,090	0.2	cocoa, copra, bananas, hardwoods, fish

Sources: *The World Almanac and Book of Facts 1995*, Funk and Wagnalls Corporation and World Population Data Sheet of the Population Reference Bureau, Inc.

The islands in this region are scattered across the Pacific Ocean. What resources and major industries do Australia and New Zealand have? What are the resources of the smaller islands of the region?

---

warm and winters are mild. Snow usually falls only in the mountains. South Island has a bit more variety. Rain clouds stop at the mountains in the west. The east can be dry.

As in Australia, the remoteness of New Zealand has led to the development of a variety of unusual wildlife. Before people came to the land, there were only a few large animals, two kinds of bats, and about 30 kinds of reptiles. One of these was the tuatara. The tuatara is the only remaining species left of an order of reptiles that died out 60 million years ago.

There are few large deposits of natural resources in New Zealand. However, New Zealand has developed hydroelectricity and **geothermal energy**. You'll remember from Chapter 1 that hydroelectricity is created by rushing water. Geothermal energy is created from steam trapped deep in the earth. Geysers release this steam naturally. The steam can also be used to drive a turbine to produce electricity.

New Zealand also is known around the world for its lamb and sheep products. New Zealand keeps most of what it grows, though. Because it is so far from other countries, it has had to learn to become self-sufficient.

The People of Australia and New Zealand

Australia's First People The first people known to have lived on these islands are called *Aborigines*. The Europeans gave them this name, which means "first people."

The Aborigines came to Australia at least 40,000 years ago from Southeast Asia. Traditionally, they are nomads who hunt and gather food. One tool that the Aborigines invented and used for hunting is the boomerang. A boomerang is a flat, curved object that is thrown at an animal. It is designed so that it returns to the thrower if it does not hit anything.

New Zealand's First People The Maoris are the first people known to live in New Zealand. They came from Polynesia, paddling to the islands in canoes. When they reached New Zealand in about A.D. 750, the Maoris named it *Aotearoa*—"the long white cloud." The Maoris lived in groups descended from common ancestors. They grew crops such as sweet potatoes.

Europeans Arrive In the 1600s, Europeans began to explore Australia and New Zealand. Once the Europeans arrived, the life of the people on these islands began to change.

One of the first Europeans to sail to New Zealand was a Dutchman. In 1642, Abel Tasman saw smoke and sent two boats ashore. Before they arrived, the Maoris set out from the beach to meet them. Wearing white feathers in their hair, the Maoris attacked Tasman's boats, killing four men. Tasman then fired on the Maoris. The boats returned to the ship. Tasman called the place "Murder's Bay." More than a century passed before the Europeans returned.

In 1768, James Cook set out from England on a three-year journey to explore the Pacific. He explored Australia as well and claimed it for Britain. Cook spent more than a year mapping Australia's east coast. He recorded the wildlife and plants he found there. He also tried to make contact with the Aborigines. According to Cook, the Aborigines

The Aborigines are the first people known to have lived in Australia. The man at the left is playing a didgeridoo, an instrument that is played by varying lip and tongue movements.

Chapter 8

live in a warm and fine climate, and enjoy . . . wholesome air, so that they have very little need of clothing; . . . many to whom we gave cloth, etc., left it carelessly upon the sea beach and in the woods, as a thing they had no manner of use for; in short, they seemed to set no value upon anything we gave them. . . . This, in my opinion, argues that they think themselves provided with all the necessaries of life.

Australia as a Penal Colony "Thieves, robbers, and villains, they'll send them away to become a new people at Botany Bay," went a popular song in Britain in 1790. Three years earlier, in 1787, the first ship of convicts had sailed from Britain to Botany Bay, Australia. The country was to be a **penal colony**, or a colony for prisoners.

Of that first group of 759 convicts, 568 were men and 191 were women. More than half of the convicts who were sent to the colony had been charged with minor theft. Eleven-year-old James Grace had stolen ten yards of ribbon and a pair of silk stockings. Another teenager had taken a packet of tobacco. For these crimes they were sentenced to live in Australia—a barren land thousands of miles from home.

The eight-month voyage was the longest voyage ever attempted by such a large group of people. They slept in the lower decks without light or windows. When the sea was calm, they could walk on deck. When the sea was not calm, they stayed below the deck—for days and weeks at a time. The convicts were terrified of what lay before them. As it turned out, they had reason to be frightened. Forty-eight people died on board. Those who did not die faced other horrors when the ship landed.

When the convicts arrived in Botany Bay, it was soon clear that no colony could survive there. The land was dry. The Aborigines on shore shouted "Warra, warra!" at the newcomers. That meant "Go away!"

They did. Within days, the group sailed to Port Jackson, which was to become Sydney, Australia's largest city.

The convicts began to create a colony. For years, life was a nightmare. Their crops did poorly. Cattle were stolen by the Aborigines. There was not enough food.

Year after year, life improved. More people arrived. Some were convicts. Others were people who hoped for a better life in the new land.

Section 1 Review

1. How are the lands and climates of Australia and New Zealand similar?
2. **Analyzing a Primary Source** Review James Cook's description of the Aborigines on this page. What did the Aborigines do with the gifts that Cook gave them? What cultural differences does Cook describe between the Europeans and the Aborigines?

On Assignment...

What would visitors to Australia and New Zealand want to know? Make notes about these ideas for your poster. How would you show the geography and climate of the region on a poster? What words would you use to describe them?

SECTION 2

Australia and New Zealand: From Colonies to Independent Nations

How did Australia and New Zealand become British colonies?

Australia's convicts and immigrants soon created colonies. In New Zealand, it was not until 1814 that European colonists came to stay. Samuel Marsden, who was a missionary, was the first colonist. He brought cattle and horses to New Zealand. The Maoris had never seen anything larger than a reptile. To them, the horses were huge.

Australia

By 1868, Britain had sent 160,000 convicts to Australia. As you read in Section 1, people other than convicts came as well. The British established six colonies in Australia. These colonies, however, did not get along with one another. People who belonged to one colony rarely visited people from the other colonies. This changed after 1851, however, when the Australian gold rush began. The population of Australia tripled in the 1850s as people from all over the world rushed to the island in hopes of making a fortune.

Some immigrants rejected life in the colonies. They set off into the outback. That rugged land was only for a hearty few, who were called **squatters**. The squatters did not have title to the land. They simply found an unclaimed piece of land and took it. Most tried to make a living by raising sheep.

Squatters' lives were difficult. They were often alone, poor, and in danger. Aborigines attacked the squatters. The Aborigines were angry because the squatters took their land and because they were no longer able to follow their nomadic way of life. The Aborigines stole sheep to eat and killed outback squatters and their families.

The squatters fought back, killing thousands of Aborigines. European diseases, though, took a heavier toll on the Aborigines. The Aborigines had no resistance to these diseases. Diseases that were relatively harmless to Europeans killed thousands of Aborigines. In the century after the first convicts came, the number of Aborigines fell from 300,000 to 80,000.

New Zealand

In New Zealand, the Maoris were angered and confused by many of the settlers' ways.

The Maoris are New Zealand's first people. When Europeans arrived, many Maoris died from disease. Others were killed in battles. About 320,000 Maoris live in New Zealand today.

Many settlers were farmers. The Maoris thought their plowing was killing the land. The Maoris owned land together. They had no idea of private ownership. Things worsened for the Maoris as more Europeans arrived and claimed the land.

Some of the Christian missionaries were unhappy at what was happening. They felt that the Maoris were being treated unfairly by the settlers. They asked the British to bring some order to the colony.

As a result, the Treaty of Waitangi was signed in 1840. The Maoris agreed to sell their land to the British government. In exchange, the British would bring government to New Zealand. They would also bring British protection.

Chapter 8

Soon, wars broke out. The Maoris did not understand the treaty. The Maoris fought for the land that was sold out from under them. Other land was taken illegally. In the 1860s, the discovery of gold brought many more settlers.

The British burned Maori villages and many Maoris were killed. Like the Aborigines, the Maoris had no resistance to many European diseases. Nearly 200,000 Maoris were killed by war or disease.

Once peace was established, Europeans developed thriving settlements in New Zealand. New Zealand's economy improved when it began to export dairy products and meat. These products sold for better prices than farmers could get in New Zealand. New Zealand's settlers began to enjoy prosperity.

A New Century

Differences among the six British colonies of Australia kept them separate until the late 1890s. In 1898, the six colonies met to establish a constitution. The constitution created a parliamentary form of government that was similar to Great Britain's. In 1901, the British colonies in Australia joined to become the Commonwealth of Australia. The Commonwealth functioned as an independent nation within the British Empire.

New Zealand was granted some rights to self-government in 1865. In 1893, it became the first country to give women the vote. In 1907, New Zealand was granted dominion status within the British Empire. That meant that it, too, was an independent nation within the empire.

In the 1930s, a worldwide economic depression affected Australia and New Zealand. There were fewer buyers for their products and people rioted for food and jobs. During World War II, Australia and New Zealand fought on the side of the Allied Powers, which included Great Britain, France, and the United States.

After the war, Great Britain's relationship with Australia and New Zealand changed. In 1973, Britain joined the European Union (EU). The EU helps European countries trade among themselves. New Zealand and Australia were no longer favored trade partners. Both lost a good many of their markets. In the 1970s, New Zealand sold two thirds of its dairy products to Britain. In 1988, less than one fifth of New Zealand's dairy products went to Britain.

In New Zealand, sheep outnumber people by about 20 to 1. Sheep are an important part of the nation's economy. New Zealand ranks second only to Australia in wool production.

> **On Assignment...**
>
> How might you show the history of Australia and New Zealand in a poster for tourists? What images would you show?

Australia and New Zealand looked to sell their wool and other products elsewhere. Now, Japan and other Asian markets are much more important. Japan is the biggest buyer of Australian goods today.

That connection with Asia is growing in other ways, too. Until the 1960s, Australia had a "white Australia" policy. Very few non-whites were allowed to settle in the country. That ended in 1973. Today almost a third of the immigrants to the country are Asian. The face of Australia is changing.

Section 2 Review

1. How did the EU change trading practices in Australia and New Zealand?
2. **Identifying Effects** What was the effect of European settlement on the Maoris and Aborigines?

SECTION 3

Oceania: A World of Pacific Islands

What is life like on the Pacific Islands?

> I should like to rise and go
> Where the golden apples grow;
> Where below another sky
> Parrot islands anchored lie.

Scotsman Robert Louis Stevenson wrote that as a young man. He later traveled to Oceania and found the world of his dreams: white beaches with palm trees swaying, bright blue skies, calm green water. To someone who was used to the gray winters of Great Britain, this was paradise. Even today, when many people think of paradise, this is what they mean.

Three Main Groups

Oceania covers a huge area of the Pacific Ocean that extends from Japan to South America. Within this area lie about 25,000 islands. The islands are grouped into three areas, as you can see on the map on page 83.

Polynesia means "many islands." This area forms a rough triangle from Hawaii to New Zealand to Easter Island. It is a huge area of about 15 million square miles (39 billion sq km).

Micronesia means "tiny islands." This area stretches west from Polynesia and north of the equator. It includes the islands north of New Guinea.

Melanesia means "black islands." Melanesia includes the islands south of the equator and west of Polynesia. New Guinea is part of Melanesia.

Climate

All of the islands in Oceania are near the equator. Because the temperature of the Pacific Ocean in this region varies very little, there is little change in air temperature on the islands from one season to another. The average temperature is near 80°F (26°C). In addition, this part of the Pacific often has severe storms called *typhoons*. South Asia, as you read in Chapter 1, has severe storms called *cyclones*.

Low Islands and High Islands

The Pacific islands fall into two groups, the "high" islands and the "low" islands. The "high" islands are usually larger. They are the tops of underwater mountains or volcanoes that have been built up from the ocean floor. These islands contain more fertile land and support more people. The people who

Palm trees sway in the breeze on this beach in Tahiti, a popular tourist spot in Oceania. Look on the map on page 83. In which of the three main island groups is Tahiti located?

live on them have a higher standard of living than their "low"-island neighbors.

There are several reasons for this. First, "high" islands get more rainfall because their mountains catch the winds. The rainy hillsides are covered with forests that can be used to build boats and houses. Because of the rain and their fertile soil, a great variety of crops are grown: rice, yams, corn, coconuts, bananas, tobacco, and taro. Taro is a starchy root plant that is made into a pastelike food called poi. The people on the "high" islands live in the valleys. Each valley supports a village. The larger islands have cities. Many of the people also raise pigs or cattle to use for food along with the fish and fruit that are native to the region. The people grow what they need for themselves; there is little to be sold.

The "low" islands are usually coral reefs, or **atolls**. Many atolls barely reach above the surface of the water. The atolls are chains of small coral islands that have been formed by millions of tiny coral animals that live in the ocean. These animals produce a limy shell that hardens to form the atoll. In the center of the atoll is a lagoon, which is a shallow body of water like a lake or pond. The coral reefs protect the lagoons by breaking the heavy ocean waves.

Life on the "low" islands is much harder than on the "high" islands. There is little or no drinking water. The soil is thin, because much of it is washed away or broken up by wind and waves. Many people live on their own small farms. They use simple digging sticks to plant their crops. Their chief food crops are coconuts, taro, and yams. They also catch fish.

On both the "high" and "low" islands, the coconut palm is a chief resource. It provides food, clothing, and shelter. For the outside world, it is a source of *copra,* or dried coconut meat. Oil is pressed from the copra to make margarine, cooking and salad oils, fine soaps, and cosmetics.

The large continental islands have most of the minerals in Oceania. Oil, gold, nickel, and copper are some of the minerals that have been found in islands such as New Guinea. Today, Papua New Guinea (the country in the eastern part of the island) receives 80 percent of its export income from copper and gold. The volcanic and coral islands have few, if any, minerals.

Oceania: Land of Many Cultures

The first people to settle Oceania were probably nomads from Southeast Asia. They reached Australia about 40,000 years ago.

After thousands of years, some moved to other islands in Melanesia.

The other islanders seem to have come from a variety of places. Some may have come from Asia in huge canoes. There are tales of Pacific Islanders who can taste the sea water and tell if they are closer to Tonga than to Fiji.

Scientists who study the population of Oceania agree that the Melanesian islands were probably the first to be inhabited. Then people went north to Micronesia. Last, people settled Polynesia.

There are few ideas that all Oceanic peoples share. One is the idea that land should be owned in common. People take only what they need from the land.

There are many cultures in Oceania. There are hundreds of different groups in Melanesia. In New Guinea, between 600 and 700 languages are spoken. The groups in these islands often did not trust one another. That led to the development of separate cultures.

Another explanation of the many cultures in Oceania is that there are many islands. With few outside influences, these groups developed their own ways of looking at the world.

The first nonnatives to come to Oceania were explorers. They came as early as the 1500s and spread the word about the islands' stunning beauty. By the 1700s, the French and English claimed islands. Missionaries came to convert the islanders to Christianity. They made little progress—until traders and settlers appeared. Some Oceanic people converted to Christianity to gain missionary support to protect their islands.

Settlers came anyway, though. They formed plantations and set up governments. They established fueling stops for trading and for warships. The islanders did what they could to ignore these settlers.

By the 20th century, almost every island had been claimed by a major power. Sometimes, the islanders benefited. They received schooling and health care. More often, the Europeans simply took the land and offered nothing in return.

During World War II, the Japanese took over many Pacific islands. The Western powers fought bloody battles over these islands. Since the war, nine islands have become independent countries. Some are linked with other countries. One of these is Hawaii, which became the fiftieth U.S. state.

Today, the South Pacific Forum speaks for the nations in Oceania. The 15-nation group has protested and ended most nuclear testing in the region. The forum has also dealt with environmental issues. One issue has been global warming. Another has been fishing nets that trap and destroy everything they catch.

The islands of Oceania continue to lure tourists with their warm climate, beautiful beaches, and tropical breezes. In recent years, islanders have begun to grow new crops to make a living. There is more mining. More timber is being cut. Oceania continues to be one of the most beautiful places on earth. Its distance from other parts of the world may help it to stay that way for many years.

> **On Assignment...**
> What kinds of images come to mind when you think of Oceania? Write those images and try to use them on your posters.

Section 3 Review

1. Why are there so many different cultures in Oceania?
2. **Comparing and Contrasting** Explain the similarities and differences between "high" and "low" islands.

Case Study 8

The Aborigines: Caught Between Two Worlds

This is a story from the Dreamtime. One night, women went to dig for yams. Those who did not find any yams felt ashamed. They flew to the sky. Then those who found yams decided to go, too. Today, all those women are stars. Those who found yams twinkle brightly. Those who did not are dim in the sky.

Life began in the Dreamtime, the Aboriginal people of Australia believe. It was a time when nature and people became one. Aboriginal peoples have been on the land for at least 40,000 years. The Dreamtime dates from that time.

During the thousands of years since, the number of Aborigines shrank. Today, Aborigines are about 1.5 percent of Australians.

Those who remain are caught between worlds. One is the world of the ancients. In that world, the land is mother and spirit. The people know the animals. They know every path and stream. Their art, which is drawn in caves, keeps the power of the Dreamtime alive.

About half of the Aborigines live in the other world. In this world of the city, Aborigines often live in very poor areas. The streets are dirt. Their houses are shacks. Today, an Aborigine in Australia can expect to live 56 years. Other Australians live an average of more than 70 years. The death rate for Aborigine babies is three times that of other Australian babies. Six times more Aborigines are out of work.

During Australia's bicentennial in 1988, 15,000 Aborigines marched on Sydney to protest. This was the anniversary of 200 years of ill treatment. Australians did more than just take land. The marchers said they treated Aborigines as sub-human.

That is changing. In 1993, the Australian High Court made an important ruling. Until then, Australia's law had said that until the Europeans came, no one lived in the country. The court ruled in 1993 that the Aborigines had been there first. The court also said that the Aborigines could claim unused land. That may mean that more Aborigines can claim land that belonged to their people thousands of years ago.

Case Study Review

1. What is the Dreamtime?
2. **Analyzing Information** How will the 1993 ruling affect Aborigines?

REVIEWING CHAPTER 8

I. Reviewing Vocabulary
Match each word on the left with the correct definition on the right.

1. outback
2. atoll
3. geothermal energy
4. geyser

a. energy produced by the earth's heat
b. dry lands of Australia where there are few settlers
c. a small coral island
d. a natural spring of hot water

II. Understanding the Chapter
Answer the questions below on a separate sheet of paper.

1. What are the main physical regions of Australia?
2. What were two effects of European settlement on the Aborigines and Maoris?
3. What are the three main divisions of the Pacific islands?
4. Why did 15,000 Aborigines march on Sydney in 1988?

III. Building Skills: Reading a Map
Use the map of Australia, New Zealand, and Oceania on page 83 to answer these questions. Write your answers on another sheet of paper.

1. Where is Australia in relation to the equator?
2. Which of the three island groups takes up the most ocean area?
3. What sea lies between Australia and New Zealand?
4. About how many miles is it from Australia to the Samoas?

IV. Working Together
Work with a group of four classmates. Imagine that the year is 1853 and you are in Australia. You will each take one of the following roles: an Aborigine, a squatter who lives in the outback, a convict from Britain, and a gold seeker. Use library resources and your text to find out as much as you can about your person's life. Then prepare a dialogue for a talk show that features the four Australians.

On Assignment...
Creating Posters: Sketch a design and decide on the captions that you will use with each picture on your two posters. Now find pictures to use, or draw your own. Assemble your posters into a display that will attract tourists to Australia, New Zealand, and Oceania. Make sure that your display has headlines. Finally, put up your display. Be ready to answer questions about this region of the world.

SOUTH ASIA

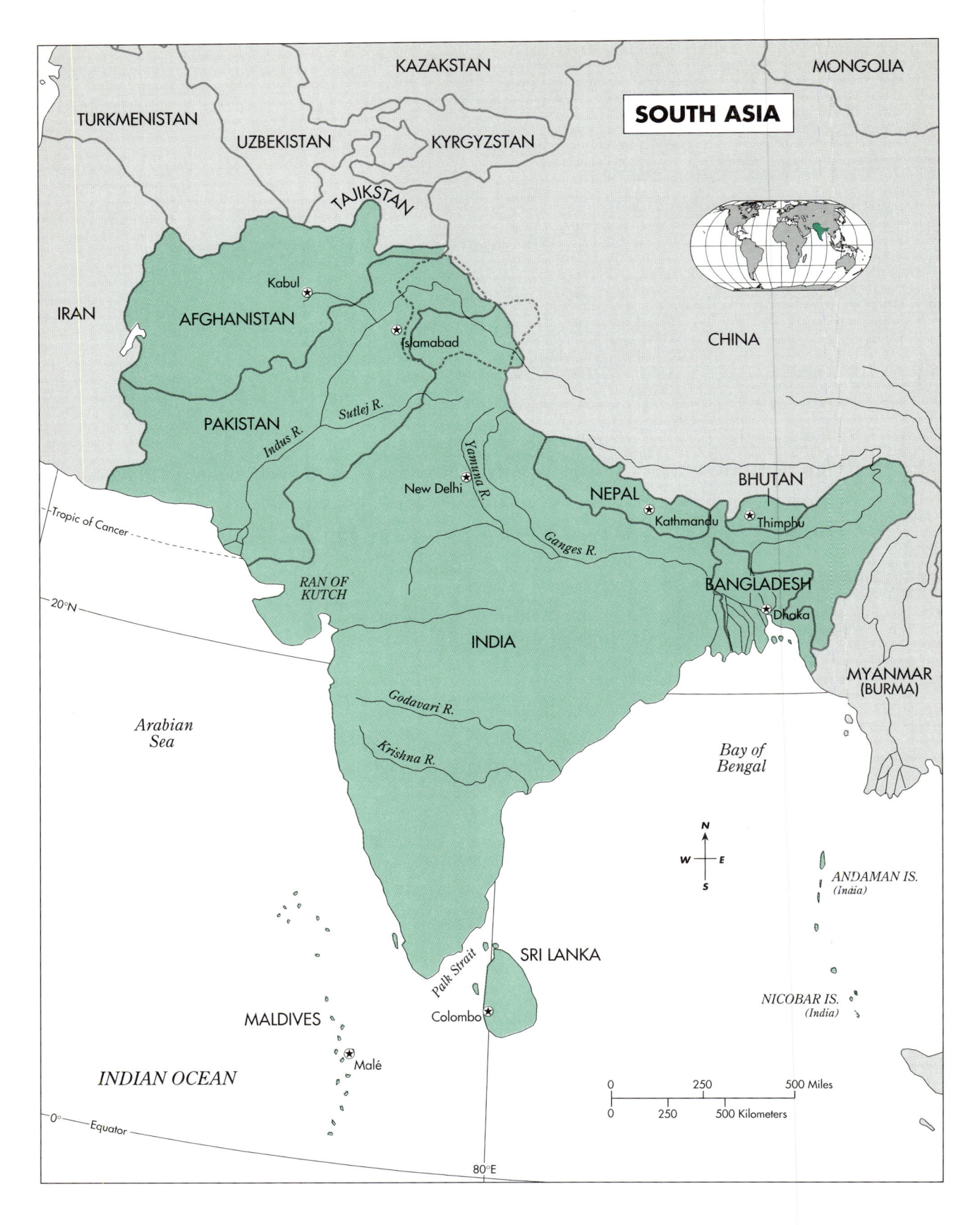

Map of South Asia

Map of Southeast Asia

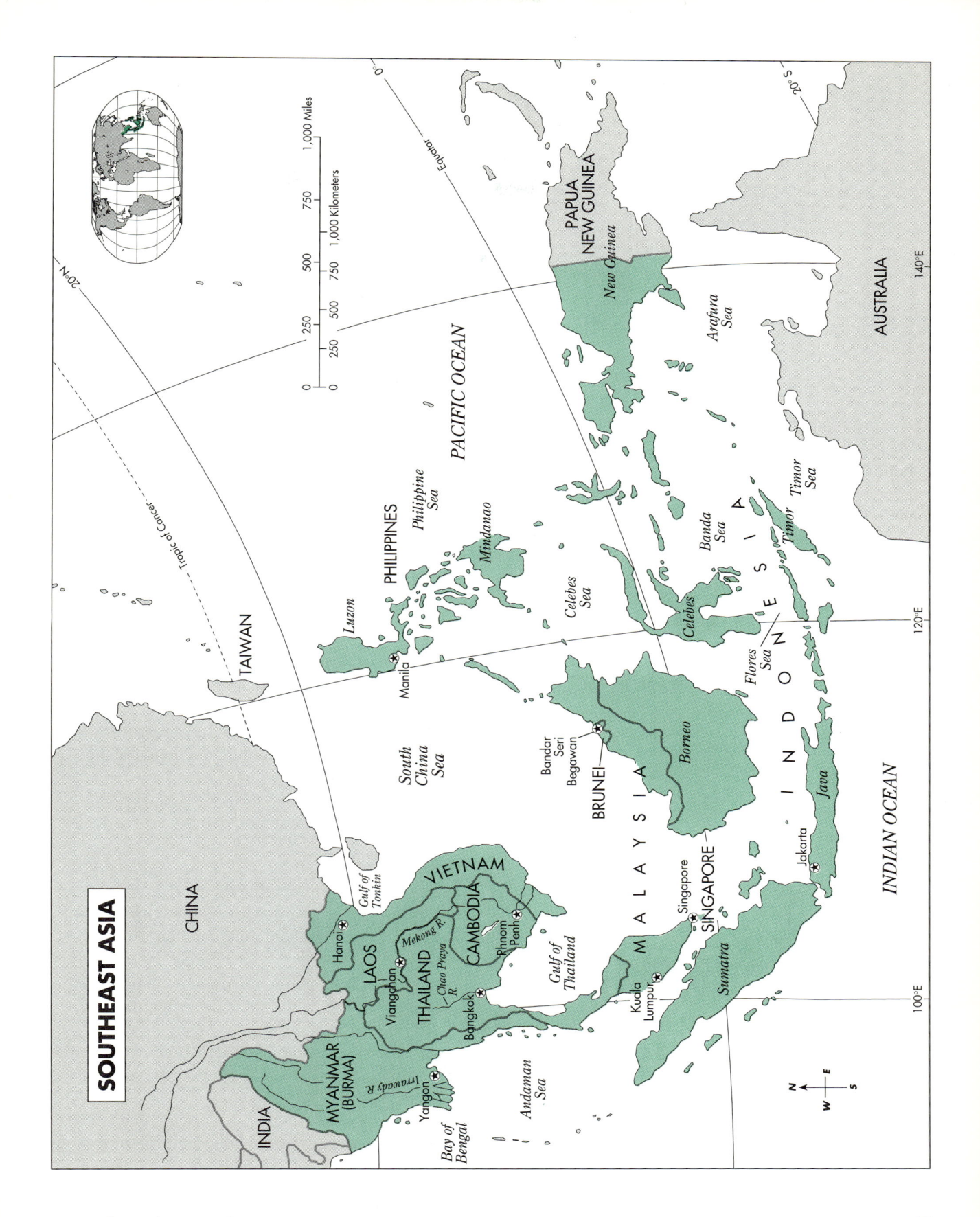

GLOSSARY

animism the belief that spirits live in the natural world in such things as rocks, trees, and streams

atoll a small coral island with a body of water at its center; most often found in the South Pacific

bustee a poor area of a city where people live in shacks

canal a ditch made by humans to carry water

capitalism an economic system in which businesses are owned privately

caste a social group based on birth; the system that separates Hindus by class and job

civil disobedience a person's refusal to follow laws that he or she believes are unjust

colony a land that is controlled by another country

communism an economic system in which the government owns and controls most property and industry

consensus an agreement reached by a group as a whole or by a majority

coup a revolt, often by military leaders, against a nation's government

cultural diffusion the spread of new ideas and new ways of doing things from one society to others

cultural diversity having a variety of cultures

culture the way of life of a group of people, including their ideas, customs, skills, and arts

cyclone a dangerous windstorm; often one that brings rain

delta a triangle of land that forms where a river meets the sea

descendant a person who can trace his or her heritage to an individual or group

dialect a regional form of a language that has its own words, expressions, and pronunciations

epic a long poem that tells the story of a hero

epidemic an outbreak of disease

extended family the family unit in most traditional societies, consisting of three or four generations of a family living in one household

geothermal energy energy produced from heat within the earth

geyser a natural spring of hot water that shoots steam or hot water into the air from time to time

gilded covered with a thin layer of gold

global village a term that refers to the entire modern world where diverse people communicate, share experiences, and depend on one another for resources

gong a round musical instrument that is struck

guerrilla warfare hit-and-run attacks by small bands of fighters against a larger power

hydroelectricity the power that comes from the force of rushing water

incense material that makes a scent when burned

insecticide a chemical that kills insects

interdependent the state of being dependent on one another for support or survival

investors people who put money into businesses in hopes of making a profit

kampung a village

market economy a system in which prices are based on what people are willing to pay and companies make goods based on what people want to buy

martial law temporary rule by the military

meditate to think deeply

migrate to move from one place to another

militant a person who believes in using violence to promote a cause

monsoon a seasonal wind that brings wet or dry weather

mosque a place of worship for Muslims

neutrality a policy of refusing to take sides in a conflict

nirvana a state in which a person has achieved perfect happiness because he or she wants nothing

non-alignment a policy of not being allied with other nations on a regular basis, but of deciding each question of foreign policy individually

nuclear family the family unit in most developed societies, consisting often of a father, mother, and children

outback the dry lands of Australia where there are few settlers

pact an agreement

penal colony a colony for prisoners

percussion instrument a musical instrument that is played by striking it

plateau a flat area that is higher than the land that surrounds it

raga one of the ancient melody patterns of Indian music

reincarnated reborn

revolt an uprising

rigid stiff; tightly controlled

squatter someone who settles on land without the right to do so

stupa a dome-shaped burial mound that serves as a Buddhist holy site

subcontinent a large landmass that juts out from a continent

Glossary

INDEX

Aborigines, 85-86, 87, 92
Afghanistan, 50
Akbar, 27
Ali Jinnah, Muhammad, 46
Ali Khan, Liaquat, 49-50
Anawrahta, King, 54
Angkor Kingdom, 54-55
Angkor Wat, 55, 69
Animism, 56
Aquino, Benigno, 76
Aquino, Corazon, 76
Arts, 67-68
Aryans, 19, 22
Asoka, 26
Association of Southeast Asian Nations (ASEAN), 77-78
Atolls, 90
Australia, 82-83, 84, 85-86, 87, 88-89, 92
Ayutthaya Kingdom, 55

Babur, 27
Bali, 57, 65-66
Bangkok, Thailand, 14, 17, 74
Bangladesh, 13, 16, 34, 47, 49
Batik, 68
Bhagavad-Gita, 23
Bhopal, 36
Bhutan, 34, 48
Bhutto, Ali, 51
Bhutto, Benazir, 51
Bombay, India, 37
Borneo, 15, 56
Brahmans, 22
Brahmaputra River, 12
Britain, 27-29, 47, 59, 60, 87, 88-89, 91
Brunei, 15, 56, 72, 77
Buddha (Siddhartha Gautama), 23-24
Buddhism, 23-25, 38, 54, 56, 66
Burma. *See* Myanmar
Bustees, 37

Cambodia, 14, 54-55, 56, 58, 61, 69, 72, 79
Canals, 29, 55
Capitalism, 72
Caste system, 22, 23

Cenaculo, 67
Ceylon. *See* Sri Lanka
Chakkri, Pya, 55
Chandragupta, 26
Chao Phraya River, 14
China, 49, 54, 78
Christianity, 26, 28, 56, 87, 91
Cities, 14, 17, 37, 74-75
Civil disobedience, 29, 36
Climate, 13, 14, 18, 82, 83-84, 89-90
Coal, 44
Colonies, 58
Communism, 48-49, 61, 73, 75-76, 78, 79
Congress party (India), 29, 30, 42, 43, 46
Consensus, 65
Constitutional monarchy, 75
Cook, James, 85-86
Cotton, 28, 44
Coup, 51
Cyclones, 13, 89

Dalai Lama, 49
da Gama, Vasco, 58
Dalang, 67
Dance, 38, 57, 68
Deccan Plateau, 13
Delhi sultanate, 27
Delta, 14
Desai, Morarji, 42
Descendants, 22
Dharma, 22
Dialect, 19
Diem, Ngo Dinh, 61
Domino theory, 61
Dragon King, 48
Dravidians, 19, 22
Drought, 42

Earthquakes, 15
East India Company, 27-28
Education, 29, 37, 64, 66
Environment, 36, 74
Epic, 38, 67
Epidemics, 36
Ethnic groups, 19, 42-43

European Economic Community (EEC), 88

Family, 66
Family planning, 36
Farming, 73
    British and, 28, 29
    canals for, 29, 55
    crops, 13, 28, 65, 74, 82, 90
    Green Revolution, 74
    in northern plain, 12-13
    problems in, 44
    rice, 11, 13, 18, 64-65, 74
    soil, 14
Festivals, 65-66
Fiji, 84
Five Pillars of Islam, 25
Four Noble Truths, 24
France, 27, 58, 59, 60

Gamelan music, 68
Gandhi, Indira, 35, 42, 43
Gandhi, Mohandas K., 29-31
Gandhi, Rajiv, 43
Ganges River, 12, 16
Geothermal energy, 84
Geysers, 83
Ghat Mountains, 13
Gilded, 68
Gongs, 67, 68
Government, 42-43, 65, 75-76
Green Revolution, 74
Guerrilla warfare, 59-60, 61
Gupta Empire, 26

Hawaii, 91
Himalaya Mountains, 10, 11, 12, 13
Hinduism, 16, 19, 22-23, 38, 43, 46, 54, 56
Hindu Kush Mountains, 12, 22
Ho Chi Minh, 61
Ho Chi Minh City (Saigon), Vietnam, 14
Housing, 65, 75
Hydroelectricity, 18

Incense, 67
India, 12, 13, 16
    arts and literature in, 38
    British rule of, 27-29
    caste system in, 23
    cities in, 36-37
    early civilizations of, 22
    economy of, 44, 49
    education in, 29, 37
    empires of, 26-27
    environmental problems in, 36
    foreign policy of, 49
    government of, 42-43
    independence of, 29-31, 46
    population of, 34, 35-36
    social change in, 34-35
    See also South Asia
Indonesia, 16, 56, 57, 60, 66, 68, 72, 74, 77
Indus River, 10, 12
Industry, 44, 72-73, 77
Insecticides, 74
Investors, 77
Irrawaddy River, 14
Islam, 16, 19, 25, 26-27, 38, 43, 46, 56, 66

Jainism, 25
Japan, 59-60, 77, 91
Java, 56, 74
Jayavarman, King, 54

Kampung, 64-65
Karma, 22
Kashmir, 42, 46
Khan, Ayub, 46
Khyber Pass, 12
Khymer empire, 69
Koran, 25
Krishna, 23
Kulintang (gongs), 68
Kumaratunga, Chandrika, 48

Lagoons, 90
Languages, 19
Laos, 14, 19, 56, 58, 72, 75, 77
Lee Kuan Yew, 73

Literature, 38, 68
Logging, 36

Mahabharata, 23, 38
Mahayana Buddhism, 25
Majapahit Kingdom, 56
Malacca, Strait of, 58
Malaysia, 15, 16, 19, 56, 59-60, 66, 72, 77
Maldives, 34
Maoris, 85, 87-88
Maranaos, 54
Marcos, Ferdinand, 76
Market economy, 73
Marsden, Samuel, 87
Marshall Islands, 84
Martial law, 42, 46, 60
Maurya Empire, 26
Meditation, 23
Mekong River, 14
Melanesia, 89, 91
Micronesia, 84, 89, 91
Migration, 54
Militants, 43
Military rule, 76
Missionaries, 26, 56, 87, 91
Mogul Empire, 27
Mongkut, King, 58
Mongols, 27, 55
Monsoons, 13, 15
Mosques, 27, 43
Mountains, 11, 12, 13, 15
Mount Everest, 11, 48
Movies, 39
Muhammad, 25
Music, 38, 68
Muslim League, 46
Muslims. *See* Islam
Myanmar (Burma), 14, 54, 56, 59, 72, 76
Myths, 57

Natural resources
    in Australia and New Zealand, 82-83
    in Oceania, 91
    in South Asia, 13, 44
    in Southeast Asia, 15
Nehru, Jawaharlal, 42, 49

Nepal, 34, 48
Netherlands, 60
Neutrality, 49
New Caledonia, 84
Ne Win, 59
New Zealand, 83-85, 86-89
Nirvana, 24, 25
Non-alignment, 49
Northern plain, 12-13
Nuclear weapons, 49, 50

Oceania, 84, 89-91
Outback, 82

Pact, 49
Pagan Kingdom, 54
Pakistan, 16, 25, 30, 34, 42, 45-47, 49-51
Papua New Guinea, 84, 91
Parliament, 42
Penal colony, 86
Peninsula, 10
Percussion instruments, 68
Persian Gulf War, 50
Philippines, 15, 54, 56, 59, 67, 68, 72, 76, 77, 78
Plateaus, 13, 14
Pol Pot, 61, 79
Polynesia, 84, 89, 91
Population growth, 35-36
Portugal, 27, 47, 58
Premadasa, Ranasinghe, 48
Punjab, 26, 42-43
Puppets, 67

Raga, 38
Railroads, 29
Rain forests, 15
Ramayana, 38
Ramos, Fidel, 76
Rao, P.V. Narasimha, 43
Ray, Satyajit, 39
Reincarnation, 23
Religion
    in South Asia, 16, 22-27, 38, 43, 45, 46
    in Southeast Asia, 19, 54, 56, 67

Index 99

Revolt, 54
Rice, 11, 13, 18, 64-65, 74
Rivers, 12, 14
Rizal, José, 68
Russia, 78

Salween River, 14
Samoa (Western), 84
Sanskrit, 22, 38
Sepoy Rebellion, 28
Shastri, Lal Bahadur, 42
Sikhs, 25-26, 42-43
Singapore, 15, 58, 60, 65, 66, 72, 73, 77
Sinhalese, 47
Solomon Islands, 84
South Asia
  geography of, 10-13, 14
  people of, 16-17, 19
  religion in, 16, 22-27, 38, 43, 45, 46
  See also specific countries
Southeast Asia
  arts and literature in, 67-68
  colonization of, 58-59, 72
  culture of, 64-66
  early civilizations of, 54-56
  economy of, 72-75
  foreign investment in, 76-77
  geography of, 13-14, 15
  government in, 75-76
  independence movements in, 59-61
  people of, 16-17, 19
  religion in, 19, 54, 56, 67
  trade with, 76-77
  See also specific countries
South Pacific Forum, 91
Soviet Union, 48, 49, 50, 75, 78
Spice trade, 58
Squatters, 87
Sri Lanka, 34, 43, 47-48
Sri Vijaya empire, 56
Stevenson, Robert Louis, 89
Stupa, 38
Subcontinent, 10, 13
Suharto, 60
Sukarno, 60
Sumatra, 55-56

Tagore, Rabindranath, 38
Taj Mahal, 27, 38
Taksin, Pya, 56
Tamil language, 38
Tamils, 47, 48
Taro, 90
Tasman, Abel, 85
Temples, 38, 55, 68, 69
Thailand, 14, 17, 55, 59, 66, 68, 72, 74, 75, 77
Thar Desert, 13
Theravada Buddhism, 25
Tibet, 49
Tibodi, Rama, 55
Trade, 27, 58, 76-77
Typhoons, 89
United Nations, 49
United States, 49-50, 61, 78
Upanishads, 23

Vanuatu, 84
Vedas, 22, 23
Vietnam, 14, 54, 56, 58, 61, 66, 72, 75-76, 77, 78
Vietnam War, 61, 78
Villages, 17, 34, 64-65
Vindhya Mountains, 13
Volcanoes, 15

Wayang kulit (shadow plays), 67
Women, 34-35, 51, 66, 68
World War I, 29
World War II, 29-30, 44, 59-60, 77, 88, 91

Yangon (Rangoon), Myanmar, 14

Zia, General, 47, 51
Zia, Begun Khalid, 47